Lets Mediate

A teachers' Guide to Peer Support and Conflict Resolution Skills for all Ages

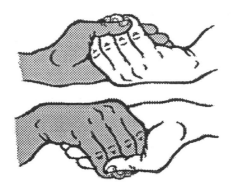

by

Hilary Stacey and Pat Robinson

©**Lucky Duck Publishing**
34 Wellington Park
Clifton
Bristol BS8 2UW
Phone or Fax 0117 973 2881 or 01454 776620
e-mail luckyduck@dial.pipex.com

ISBN 1 873942 71 0

Acknowledgments

We would like to thank the following people:

Peer Mediators of all ages who have taught us so much

Murray White and the Self Esteem Network

The Ulster Quaker Peace Education Project

The Kingston Friends Workshop Group

The European Network for Conflict Resolution in Education (ENCORE)

Mildred Masheder

LEAP Confronting Conflict Project

The West Midlands Quaker Peace Education Project

The Saltley Plus Consortium of Schools

Dr. Peter Silcock, Nene College

Mediation UK

Professor Tim Brighouse, (Birmingham Chief Education Officer) and

Louise Hughes, (Birmingham Schools Advisor)

Daniel Cremin and Chris Robinson

Preface

Conflict is neither good nor bad, conflict just is! Attitudes towards conflict vary, from those who avoid it at all costs to those who positively seek it out, but the fact remains that it is an unavoidable part of life. It is the way that the conflict is dealt with that determines the outcomes. If dealt with in a way that respects the rights of all involved, it can be a motivator for positive change and even for transformation (Crum, 1987). Pupils need to be taught effective conflict resolution skills as part of their training for citizenship and as part of learning to deal with situations of conflict and bullying in school. If this is not done, we are in danger of unconsciously handing on to them attitudes towards conflict that may not be helpful as they face the challenges of the next century.

This book contains ideas and activities that can culminate with pupils offering a peer mediation service to help them resolve each others conflicts.

Just as important, and just as much fun, are the activities that develop the skills of affirmation, co-operation, effective communication and listening, which are needed for mediation. They can be used as part of personal and social education, and many of them can be used to teach the core curriculum.

Contents

 denotes a copiable handout

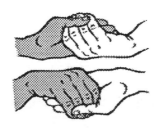

Chapter 1
Mediation in Schools

What is mediation?

Mediation is a structured process in which a neutral third party assists voluntary participants in resolving their dispute.

Mediation is not about deciding who is right or wrong, or apportioning blame, or even focusing on the past any more than is necessary to help the disputants to work out the way forward in the future. Mediators do not offer any advice but instead assist the disputants to find mutually acceptable solutions.

Mediation allows the disputants to:

- define the problem from their point of view
- identify and express their feelings and needs
- hear the feelings and needs of the other person
- acknowledge each other's point of view
- create solutions
- agree a course of action
- evaluate progress and repeat if necessary.

This is all done in a safe and structured environment, managed and controlled by the mediator. Agreed ground rules are laid down which the disputants must accept.

Where is Mediation Happening?

Mediation is now growing in the UK. It is used for neighbourhood disputes, commercial disputes, environmental disputes, and situations where offenders ask to use mediation to make some form of reparation to their victim. There are almost one hundred neighbourhood mediation services, funded by charities or local authorities. It is also used in divorce proceedings to resolve issues of finance and access to children before court proceedings.

The philosophy behind mediation came from the United States about twenty years ago and has influenced other fields. It can be traced in management training, assertiveness training (Dickson, 1989), in the peace movement (Curle, 1987), positive parenting initiatives, in the principles and practice of humanistic counselling (Rogers, 1951) and in some forms of psychotherapy including transactional analysis (Harris, 1973). The philosophy behind this approach to conflict is one that more and more people are discovering and applying in a variety of ways.

Teaching Mediation in Schools

What of the roots and practice of mediation in schools? Mediation thrives in an atmosphere of:

- positive relationships
- trust
- support
- open communication
- mutual respect
- tolerance
- co-operation
- readiness to work through problems.

It cannot work in an atmosphere of:

- negative relationships
- mistrust
- lack of support
- avoidance of conflict
- disrespect
- intolerance
- secrecy
- aggressive confrontation.
- you-do-it-because-I-say-so management or teaching styles

If you recognise your school in the second list and are beginning to despair, take heart. If there is at least a willingness from certain key members of staff to try new approaches, mediation can help to effect a culture change in school.

There have been many initiatives in education over the past few years that have been based on a similar value-system. A greater emphasis on group-work and problem solving has improved young people's ability to co-operate. More individualised and autonomous learning have taught young people to have a more internal locus of control. A focus on speaking and listening skills has improved pupils' ability to communicate, and a growing awareness of the importance of high self-esteem has meant that many schools are seeking out opportunities to affirm and acknowledge young people.

Other links can be found with initiatives such as schools councils, democratic schooling, anti-bullying interventions, peer tutoring and peer counselling, education for citizenship, world studies and Circle Time. Above all, these initiatives stress pupil empowerment. Peer mediation works primarily because it empowers young people to resolve their own disputes. It does this by equipping them with skills that will remain with them for a long time after the immediate conflict has been resolved.

In order for young people to be trained as peer mediators the skills of affirmation (the ability to recognise one's own and other people's strengths), co-operation, and communication (both speaking and listening) have to be in place.

The Iceberg Principle

Developed by the Children's Creative Response to Conflict Project - New York

Figure 1

Figure 1 shows the Iceberg Principle which was developed by the Children's Creative Response to Conflict Project in New York (Prutzman, 1988) in response to inner-city violence, and which has been used by most people working in this field in the UK as a starting point. It shows how effective problem management (problem-solving is not always possible) is merely the tip of the iceberg. The three core skills that are below the surface of the water are supporting the problem management.

By breaking each skill area down into related skills and activities an extended programme can be delivered as an ongoing part of the curriculum rather than as a brief intervention. In this way also the influence of the group can be brought to bear upon the psychology of the individual as a member of the group and in a whole school approach. The resulting changes in behaviour and attitude permeate the whole of school life.

Towards Peer Mediation

The aims of teaching mediation in schools
This list was produced by a group of Birmingham teachers in November 1993:
- to develop social skills for pupils and staff in dealing with conflict in a more positive way
- to create a calm, cooperative classroom atmosphere
- to affirm pupils and raise their self esteem
- to give pupils alternatives to disruption and violence
- to create understanding and awareness of others
- to give pupils ownership of their resolution of disputes
- to enhance learning through creating a safer, more positive environment.

Groundwork
This work always begins with foundation work in the curriculum (often through P.S.E, using "Circle Time" as a vehicle) to create a positive empowering climate and a collaborative whole group approach to:
1. ensure safety and trust (Ground rules and communication)
2. develop empathy and respect for each other and to develop a positive self image (Affirmation)
3. share and collaborate - operating successfully as a member of the class community (Co-operation)
4. express needs and feelings and identify and implement creative solutions to issues and difficulties. (Emotional intelligence and Problem-solving).

The curriculum
A spiral curriculum, where groundwork at each level is appropriate to the developmental stage of the pupils, focuses on the broad areas indicated in the iceberg. The skills and concepts which enable a non-violent, creative approach to conflict resolution are established at each phase.
For example:
- properly functioning ground rules
- taking turns to speak
- listening with respect
- accepting and including everyone
- operating as a member of a group.

Speaking and Listening Skills
- expressing individual thoughts, feelings and point of view

- accepting the validity of opposing or conflicting opinions
- developing vocabulary and using positive, assertive language.

Social and Emotional Skills
- able to affirm others and accept affirmation
- identifying feelings so as to:
    understand your own responses
    understand causes
- develop strategies to:
    cope with feelings
    change responses
    control impulse
- developing empathy
    seeing and appreciating differing points of view
    being aware of the difference between actions and
    interpretations.

Resolution Skills
- attacking the problem and not the person
- separating issues and value judgments
- understanding and owning needs
- stating needs and wants positively
- brainstorming creative solutions.

Figure 2, page 10 shows how the curriculum work which develops the skills identified earlier in the Iceberg, closely follows the skills that pupils will need to use in the mediation process, both as disputants and as mediators.

Mediation process

Step 1. Introduction (ground rules and impartial, no blame approach).
Step 2. Hear problem and feelings (narrate problem, express feelings and needs).
Step 3. Acknowledgment and empathy. (see the other person's point of view and acknowledge his/her feelings).
Step 4. Suggestions and choices (brainstorm suggestions make offers and requests).
Step 5. Negotiation and agreement (agree a mutually acceptable way for ward).

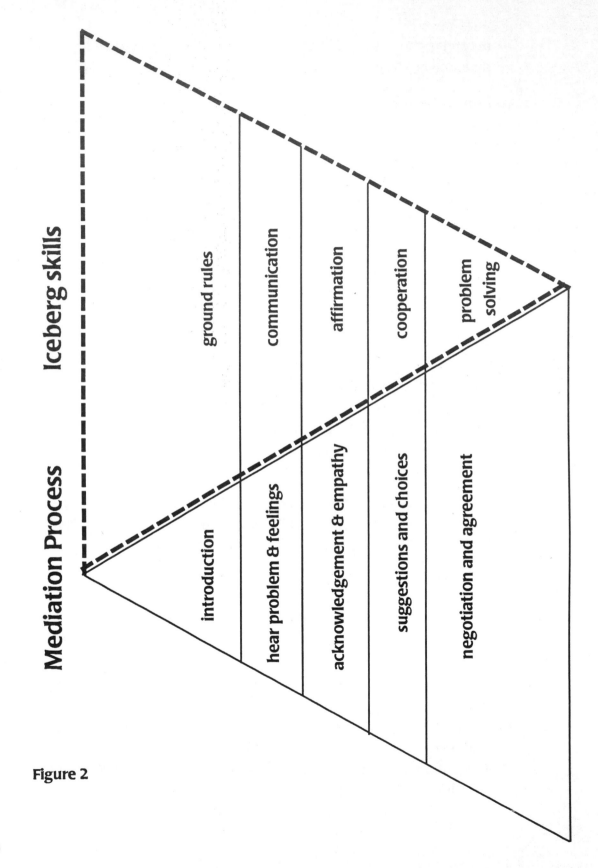

Iceberg skills

ground rules

communication

affirmation

cooperation

problem solving

Mediation Process

introduction

hear problem & feelings

acknowledgement & empathy

suggestions and choices

negotiation and agreement

Figure 2

The development of Peer Mediation and pro-social skills at different phases

Nursery / Infant
Nursery / Infant children need practise in essential pro-social skills, with rehearsal of speaking and listening skills, taking turns and controlling impulse. As this stage foundation work on positive self image develops confidence and high self esteem, both fundamental pre-requisites for resolving disputes positively.

Top infants
Infant disputants can hear each other's side of the story and feelings and agree what to do for the best. Top infant mediators can use a simplified process as mediators.

Juniors - Years 3 - 4
Juniors need to continue positive self image building and receive support to develop their emerging sense of "self" as a member of a group. They build on the speaking and listening skills of early years, developing vocabulary work to express:

- a broader range and awareness of issues and feelings
- empathy
- an understanding of cause and effect
- positive and creative responses to problems.

Junior - Years 5 and 6
Success depends upon the curriculum work already in place and the school's support for emerging independence. Year 5/6 mediators are able to help both disputants to understand what the problem is about, appreciate each others point of view, choose a way forward and make positive changes.

Secondary - Years 7 and 8
In years 7 and 8 the foundation for positive interaction can be laid through P.S.E., English, P.E. and a variety of other curriculum areas. There is a need to develop positive self-image and to establish group cohesion, empathy, respect and mutual aid. Continuing communication skills development is important particularly in relation to feelings (including impulse and anger management, asserting needs and counselling skills). They can begin creative problem solving and peer mediation.

Secondary - Years 9, 10 and 11
These years also need affirmation and self esteem work, together with greater depth to emotional intelligence work and communication skills. All year groups

are able to mediate successfully for their peers, but undoubtedly, years 10 and 11 are better able to summarise underlying issues and identify unexpressed needs for the disputants.

If older pupils are to provide a service for younger ones, it will be important to have developed other strategies to create easy reciprocal relationships between the year groups, i.e. Buddy Systems, or older pupils regularly taking some P.S.E. sessions or assemblies, running clubs or services for younger pupils, or regular opportunities for social interaction.

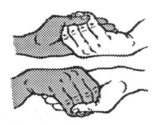

Chapter 2
How To Use This Book

The Skills

This book is based around six areas of skill:

- speaking and listening
- affirmation
- co-operation
- emotional literacy
- conflict resolution
- mediation,

at three levels:

- Beginner • Intermediate • Advanced •

These levels are not age specific. They are developmental. Everyone needs to start at the beginning and work as far towards or through the advanced activities as they are able to, and at their own pace.

For some this journey will be a slow unfurling. For others it will be a sudden flowering of latent potential and skills which have remained passive. "Suddenly I've learnt I've got skills that I never knew I had," is how one 15 year old boy mediator put it. He had surprised himself with his own talent and ability.

What matters is that young people's progress should not be limited by adult expectation. An observant teacher will know just when children are ready for the next challenge, when success is just within reach and a sense of achievement can be maximised.

When an infant school headteacher in Birmingham gave her pupils the opportunity to develop mediation techniques, (something most adults felt would be beyond their grasp), she knew they were ready for the challenge and was signalling her belief in them. Once given the opportunity they surpassed all expectation, displaying an impressive range of inter-personal skills and emotional maturity.

Use the levels in the six skill sections to match the needs of your pupils. They may be on advanced level speaking and listening skills but need to return to beginner cooperation skills for example.

The Lessons

Initially lessons will focus on establishing the ground rules within a positive, affirming atmosphere, and will concentrate on developing pro-social skills through interactive games, pair work, small group work and Circle Time.

Later when the skills base has been established, longer activities can be interspersed with the circle work and the whole process can become a vehicle for the delivery of the curriculum.

Circle Time

Circle Time is an approach that we rely on very heavily to develop pupils' speaking and listening skills. Anyone who is not familiar with Circle Time would be well advised to read one of the many excellent books about it (see the bibliography at the back of this book), or view the Lucky Duck video, "Coming Round to Circle Time".

In Circle Time the pupils sit in a circle. One pupil starts and then each pupil around the circle has a chance to make a contribution or pass. The advantage of this is that the pupils learn to speak one at a time and quieter pupils, who may find it hard to make a space to be heard, have an automatic opportunity to contribute. All contributions are treated with equal respect. This develops inclusiveness, acceptance and a whole - group approach.

An object can be used for the pupils to pass around to identify their turn to speak and to give those listening a focus or marker. This means that the speaker decides when s/he has finished and is ready for the next person to begin. The pupils know that only the person holding the object will speak and so it avoids interruptions and more than one person speaking at a time. It is important that adults also respect this convention, provided that it is safe to do so.

An affirming atmosphere is very important. Thanking pupils for contributions and warm eye-contact help build up good feelings. Focusing on the positive and giving frequent praise helps pupils feel more able to share things. Above all Circle Time should be about having fun together, sharing and valuing each other's experiences and insights and moving forward together as a whole class.

> For those not familiar with Circle Time it is essential to read about the structure and process or to join an existing group. Some suitable books and a video are recommended in the bibliography.

A Typical 30 Minute Circle Time Session

Theme - Free Time

Warm-Up
e.g. Throwing soft ball (juggling balls are ideal) across the circle to someone whilst saying good morning and their name.

Individual Go-Round
e.g. "In my free time I like to ...."

Jumbling Up Game
e.g. "I love all my friends, especially those who ...."

Pair-Work Go-Round
Children work in pairs with the person sitting next to them. After two minutes discussion time, each pair reports something back to the circle. e.g. "We both like ...." (chocolate).

Energising Game
e.g. Fives.

Individual Go-Round
e.g. "If I could do anything in my free time I would ...."

Listening Check
e.g. Five children are picked at random from the circle. Who can remember what they said they would like to do in their free time if they could do anything?

Feed-Back
Debriefing session. What worked well today? How might we do things differently next time? Did anyone go out of their way to be helpful? Are we managing to stick to the ground-rules? Which was their favourite part of the session? What did they learn today?

Ending Game
Quieter game e.g. Spontaneous Counting.

Observing and Evaluating

The exercises in this book provide the basis for a comprehensive course in conflict resolution skills. They should not be seen as a prescriptive or dogmatic set of instructions, but rather as a starting point for the teacher to make creative modifications to meet the needs of the young people in her group. The choice of activities, the starting point, and the rate of progress will vary from group to group, what is important is that the activities are appropriate and that everyone moves forward together.

Appropriate activities will be based on observations of the group as a whole. Difficulties in doing things well (e.g. all keeping the ground rules) or in mixing with others (boys with girls, outside usual friendship cliques, across cultural, racial or religious groups) problems with specific skills (speaking and listening pair work where some pupils may experience difficulty in holding a conversation or narrating experiences) are all indications of starting points and not of failure. Activities can be repeated in different ways, adding a little twist to meet the immediate needs of the group.

Teachers should not feel that they need to be responsible for providing all the solutions or answers to observed behaviours or performance. The nature of the process that the class are engaged in is such that they should be encouraged to appraise their own performance in achieving skills and to develop strategies to ensure that everyone succeeds.

Pupils of all ages are able to reflect on what they did well and to suggest what would make it even better or how to make sure that everyone is successful, provided they know what they were trying to achieve in the first place. Reasons for doing games or activities need to be made overt. Pupils can be asked, "Why are we doing this?" "What is this helping us to do?" "What skills do we need to use to play this game well?"

Evaluation should be affirming and positive, building on what is done well (however small that may seem to be initially). Success must be made achievable. It may help to break some activities down into smaller targets, with a time limit and a reward of their choosing or a game to begin or end with.

By involving the group in this process of reflection and appraisal, the seeds of problem solving, cooperation and collaborative responsibility are sown.

Linking with the Behaviour Management Policy

Clearly, the positive-relationship-building work and the problem-solving and peer mediation work cannot happen in a vacuum. The classroom culture and the wider school ethos have a vital role to play. In fact, very little progress will be made if the teaching styles are overly didactic and if the school's behaviour-management policy is entirely authoritarian and punitive, leaving young people little room to practice their skills.

Children learn far more from observing what we do than by listening to what we say. If we respond to a child who has been bullying, for example, by bullying him or her in turn (humiliating, using verbal violence), then we are modelling behaviour of which we say we disapprove. Our behaviour-management strategies must be clear, just and assertive; that is recognising our own right to teach, the pupils' right to learn and our shared right to be treated with respect.

It seems to us that current behaviour management theory and practice can be put into three broad bands for which we use the terms authoritarian, behaviourist and pupil-centred.

Whilst it will be clear by now that we favour pupil-centred approaches to behaviour-management we do not underestimate the value of the other two approaches. All three have their place and their advantages and disadvantages, as we have tried to show in the table below. We feel that adults who are serious in their intentions to help pupils become independent learners and confident autonomous young people, will be equally serious about changing their behaviour management style to suit and support their pupils' emerging independence.

Figure 3

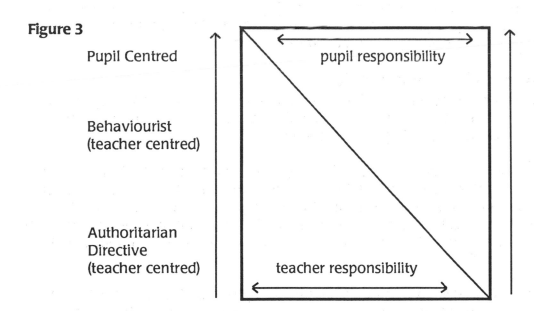

Pupil Centred

Behaviourist
(teacher centred)

Authoritarian
Directive
(teacher centred)

pupil responsibility

teacher responsibility

An authoritarian approach will be needed if a pupil uses violence in school, both that pupil and the wider community need to know that violence will always be dealt with in a firm and consistent way by those responsible for maintaining a safe school environment.

A behaviourist approach may be of value for a pupil who finds it hard to sit still and listen for long enough to participate in pupil-centred approaches.

Pupil centred approaches can be used to develop a collaborative style where pupils talk openly about issues that affect their class. It will help to create a classroom environment in which aggressive behaviour and language are counteracted by teachers and pupils, and where all pupils, even those who find it hard to sit still and listen, or to cooperate, are accepted and supported in their attempts to improve their skills.

Pupil-centred behaviour-management is a long term, on-going process, but pupils who have acquired speaking and listening skills through Circle Time can ultimately use them to create, evaluate and modify school rules, help each other to stick to them, acknowledge and reward each other's good behaviour, achievements and personal qualities, give each other tips on effective anger-management and solve problems together democratically.

Some classes that we have worked with use "agenda-boards", (that is a blank agenda pinned to the notice board at the beginning of each week which the pupils write on as and when an issue arises) or topic boxes for pupils to post suggestions into, to be used in class meetings. One Headteacher who is now four years into the process, has noted that her lunchtime "incident book" records a 50% reduction in entries since the project began.

Rights and Responsibilities

This work often begins with the pupils discussing their rights and responsibilities, the rules that they agree to abide by in the classroom and playground, and the sort of shared culture they wish to create.

The focus on responsibility as well as rights and rules means that the pupils can be given a clear message that it is not enough to avoid doing wrong. Each pupil is also responsible for ensuring that the rights of others are not infringed. In the case of bullying, for example, the pupils can be given the message that it is their responsibility not only to avoid bullying others, but also to tell a teacher if they witness bullying.

Instead of having a profusion of class rules imposed by the teacher which need constant updating and enforcing, when an incident does occur the teacher can simply ask the pupil - "Whose rights did you infringe here?" or "What responsibility did you avoid?" Pupils will be more motivated to keep to any rules that were made by them with their class.

Two examples of an end result of this process of negotiation might be as follows:

When I come to school I have:

The right to be happy and to be spoken to with respect.

The responsibility to avoid making others unhappy and putting others down.

I agree to the rule of no name-calling and put-downs, and I agree to speak to others with respect.

When I come to school I have:

The right to feel safe.

The responsibility to avoid using violence against others.

I agree to the rule of no violence.

Pupils can write out their agreed rules in a variety of ways, either as a poster that is on display in the class at all times, or individually as part of a signed contract that could also be signed by parents who wish to declare that they will support their child in keeping to them. Lunchtime supervisors can also be involved in the process and are often grateful for some agreed guidelines that help to create a school ethos that extends into lunchtimes.

Adult use of language.

Disruptive or uncooperative behaviour provides the opportunity to develop group support and to model language which attacks the issue at hand and not the individual. It is a powerful opportunity to challenge stereotyping, labelling of individuals and scapegoating, whilst promoting whole group achievement. Messages should focus on:

- the behaviour
- its effect
- the needs/wants of the group or agreed code of behaviour.

This is a formula which pupils themselves are taught as part of their conflict resolution work.

Instead of:

> "Sahida and Cheryl. Stop that whispering you silly girls. You're spoiling it for everyone else and you've broken the rules."

the message is changed to becomes a whole group appeal.....

> "Whispering (the behaviour) stops us from hearing what each person is saying (the effect) and we have agreed to listen with respect to each person because what each person has to say matters. Let's try it again."

Sahida and Cheryl's self esteem is still intact and they are reminded what is expected and why. The next successful "go-round" with everyone listening will be a cause for praise and rewarded with something which signals success. Pupils often spontaneously applaud themselves. The whispering was also an indication that Sahida and Shirley needed another minute before the "go-round" to be sure of which of them was going to say what.

A more intractable difficulty with an individual pupil would still follow the same basic process:

> "John, we like you and we want you in our circle/group but we don't like insults (the behaviour) because they are very hurtful and stop people from feeling that they can talk about things they care about (the effect). In this group we have no put downs or insults and we listen with respect to what people are saying."

If there is more than one appeal or reminder of this sort, it may be necessary to ask whether John is willing to keep the ground rule and remain with the group. If not, he is asked to leave the circle for a while, and invited to rejoin shortly after a game or happy activity.

Make success possible
Keep games, activities, "go-rounds" short and sweet. Dismantle things into achievable pieces. A successful activity is one in which the whole group has performed well.

Keep statements positive
Say what you DO want and what you ARE all working towards.

Offer challenges
Agree short goals (e.g. copy an action accurately in turn round the circle in 20 seconds and invite them to improve on it).

Reward success
A cheer, applause, a "football" clap with "We did it!" at the end, a "thank you" hand squeeze or smile passed round the circle, a choice of game, activity or song.

Above all...
Model the behaviour that you are expecting from your pupils. (Maines, B. J. and Robinson, G. S. 1988)

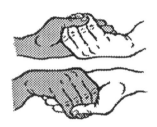

Chapter 3
Beginnings

Naming Games

These are to tie in with speaking and listening, affirmation and cooperation work. Use them as observation pointers to the skills and relationships in the group. You can tell a great deal from watching how interactive games are played by the class. Use them to build group cohesion and inclusive relationships. Use them as a preparation for mixed pair work and group work and as incentives for other work completed well.

Games help reinforce teaching points, mix pupils up, and energise or calm them down. Games can be alternated with periods of listening to break the listening time into manageable chunks..... or simply enjoyed for the fun they bring to working together.

First introductions

1. Roll or throw the ball across the circle.
2. Say your own name when you catch it. Continue until everyone has been included.
3. Do the same but this time say the name of the person you are giving the ball to.

Very young children and special needs pupils enjoy playing "Naming Goals" where they sit on the floor with their feet apart as goal posts to catch the ball as it is rolled to them. Their name is called by everyone when the ball rolls into their "goals". They can be helped to roll successfully across the circle if there are two or more people sitting back to back in the centred of the circle ready to catch the ball and pass it on to the intended goal.

An extension of this would be to call a greeting and name the person you are rolling to, who then thanks you by name.

Introducing partners round the circle

This is very worthwhile doing even if the group have been together for some time.
1. Simply say the name of the person on your right
2. Say your own name and the name of the person on your right followed

by the name of the person on your left.
3. In pairs find one piece of positive information about your partner. (Favourite game/ colour/food/ season, something they like to do in their spare time, one thing they think is good about school etc.)
4. Introduce your partner to the group and share the information.

Signing in

1. The first person says their name and adds a small gesture or sign.
2. The second person repeats the first person's name and sign and then says their own and so on round the circle with each person repeating the names and gestures of those who have gone before them.
3. As a support, the group can prompt each other by silently "signing" the names.

Saved by the bell

1. One person elects to be in the middle of the circle. To start them off they are given the name of one person sitting down.
2. They walk towards the person whose name they have been given and in order to get that person to swop places with them they touch the person on both feet.
3. When the seated person realises that the person in the middle is coming their way they "ring" for help by saying "ding" or "ring-ring" (if they have time).
4. The rest of the group can save them from having to change places by calling out their name before they are touched on the toes by the person in the middle.
5. If they are touched on the toes before anyone calls their name they swop with the person in the middle, who before sitting down whispers a name to them.
6. If they are saved by the group, the person in the middle can select a new name for themselves from anyone they heard calling out the last person's name.

Dracula

This is similar to the last game but instead of the group rescuing their classmate, the chosen "victim" calls the name of someone else in the circle to deflect "Dracula" (the person in the middle of the circle) away from them. Instead of touching toes, "Dracula" must touch the named person on both shoulders. A very popular game with 7 to 13 year olds.

Source: Mollie Curry & Caroline Bromfield (1994).

Ghost in the cupboard

1. Sitting in a circle.
2. One person goes outside.
3. One (or more) hide out of sight in the room.
4. Everyone stands up and changes places.
5. The person outside comes in and has to guess who the ghost in the cupboard is, i.e. who is missing from the circle.
6. They can ask for clues if they get stuck. Clues can be restricted to information learnt in Circle Time, or given in a particular order e.g. something they are good at, then hair or eye colour, then gender etc. Clues should always be positive and never hurtful.

I sit on the hill, with my friend......

1. One spare chair in the circle. The two people either side of the spare chair try to be first to sit on it.
2. The winner having sat on the chair says, "I sit.."
3. The person nearest the winners original (now empty) chair moves to sit on it and says, "On the hill..."
4. The person nearest the next empty chair moves onto it and says "with my friend......" and says the name of someone across the circle from them.
5. The named friend crosses the circle to sit in the chair just vacated.
6. The two people either side of the friend's chair try to be first to sit on it and the game continues with the winner saying, "I sit..."
7. When this is done quickly with no pauses to choose friends it develops a very satisfying rhythm to it. Check what they feel they are doing well (what skills do you need to be able to play this game well?) and what they suggest would improve it for everyone.

Mixing Up Games

These games are planned:
- To energise the class and bring them together.
- To mix pupils in the circle to ensure that they are not sitting in their usual friendship groups.

Pupils sitting in a circle of chairs. No special resources are needed except for Noah's Ark, which needs pairs of animal cards.

Stand up and change places if ......

The teacher (or a pupil) asks everyone to stand up and change places if .... ,
for example:
    ...you had toast for breakfast this morning
    ...you are wearing black shoes
    ...you like chocolate
    ...you have a brother.
This can be done purely as a mixing-up game, or it can be extended to help
pupils to get to know each other better by including categories of information about likes and dislikes, position in the family, where you were born,
festivals you celebrate, languages you speak, pets, pastimes and whether
you think certain things are a good idea or not.

I love all my friends especially those who .....

As "Stand up and changes place if ...." but this time one pupil stands in the
middle and their chair is taken away. The pupil says: "I love all my friends,
especially those who ....", e.g. are wearing black shoes.
Anyone with black shoes changes places and the pupil in the middle tries to
sit down also, leaving another pupil in the middle at the end whose turn it
is to begin the next go.
This can also be done (and linked into maths) by giving pupils numbers. The
pupil in the middle calls out all odd numbers, for example, or all number
under ten, or all numbers that can be divided by three, and so on.
Also pupils can be given names of fruit or anything else that fits in with a
current topic, and all the oranges, for example, can change places. If fruit
salad is called everyone changes places.
As pupils become more accustomed to their similarities and differences
being accepted, they can be invited to change the topics to include
thoughts and opinions as well as likes and dislikes.

Noah's Ark

The pupils sit in a circle and are all given a card with the name or picture of
an animal on it. There are two of each animal. They are asked to look at
their card, but not to show it to anyone. The aim of the game is for them
to move into the middle of the circle and find the other animal in their
pair by miming it whilst looking out for someone else miming the same.

When they have found their pair, they go and sit down together ready for
the teacher to go round at the end and check that all animals are correctly
paired and present! (see pages 27 - 29 for a copiable set of animal cards

to use with this game).

Another way to pair up is to use the animal sounds.

Link-ups

A variation on this is asking pupils to stand up and find others who...... live in the same street/have seen the same film/read the same book/like the same soap opera/ play the same sport, and to link arms with them. When a small group has formed they wait to be identified, before moving on to the next category.... and finally sit down together.

Human Lotto/ Someone who...

Another way of finding out about people. Decide together on 12 different categories of information you might like to know about someone before feeling you knew them really well. e.g. taste in music, hobbies, favourite food, etc. On a piece of paper write "Someone who..." and then list your own examples of each of these e.g. ..."likes pizza" ..." goes dancing" ...etc. Interview classmates to find a different person who likes each of the things on your list. Bring the lists into the circle and feedback (see page 30).

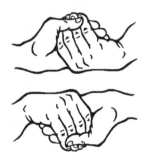

mouse	monkey
goose	fish
pig	dog
cow	penguin
frog	bee
horse	hen

List some of the things you like.
Find out who likes the same things.

I like...   and so does [   ]

I like...   and so does [   ]

I like...   and so does [   ]

I like...   and so does [   ]

I like...   and so does [   ]

I like...   and so does [   ]

I like...   and so does [   ]

I like...   and so does [   ]

I like...   and so does [   ]

I like...   and so does [   ]

Chapter 4
Speaking and Listening

It is pupils ability to stick to the basic ground rules of Circle Time that enable each individual to feel safe enough to contribute to class discussions. The language of ground rules varies, but in essence there are two - no interrupting and no put downs (which are also the two important rules that enable mediation to take place). Stated positively these become - listen with respect until it is your turn to speak.

If these rules are not adhered to by everyone, then pupils may feel exposed and open to disinterest or ridicule when talking about their thoughts or feelings to the rest of the class. The rest of the class may also feel free to contradict or add comments to the contribution of individuals.

However long it takes to establish a safe environment for open discussion to take place, it is important to avoid the temptation to move on too quickly. Trust and basic speaking and listening skills can be established through discussing relatively "safe" topics, such as favourite food or television programmes until an inclusive, respectful and supportive process is established as the norm.

When pupils are using their speaking and listening skills as a whole group, it is equally important to establish a willingness on the part of every pupil to talk with, and listen to, any other pupil in the class whilst working in pairs.

Speaking and Listening for Staff

Many staff teams have benefited from adopting a Circle Time approach to their own staff meetings. One of the major benefits is the way in which this approach treats all contributions equally and gives everyone the right to be listened to with respect.

> Circle Time speaking and listening is a positive time for pupils and adults. See adult use of language (chapter 2).
>
> Do pupils know when and where they can find a 'listening ear' if they have a problem they need to talk through?
>
> Do you listen to pupils who come to you with a problem or do you talk to them about what you think they should do?

Circle Time - A Summary

Children sit in a circle of chairs.

Ground-Rules:
- Respect for each other (no "put-downs", no deriding faces or noises).
- Only one person speaking at a time. Focused listening by those not speaking.

An object can be passed around the circle, to indicate whose turn it is to speak.

A 'go-round' is where everyone in turn makes a contribution about a particular subject,

- My favourite colour is...
- My happiest day was when
- I enjoyed studying this topic because..

A successful "go-round' is one in which everyone has kept the ground rules and participated as a member of the group.

Anyone who passes can have another go at the end when they have had more time to think.

It is often necessary to repeat some of the earlier Circle Time activities. With each new class the process of trust-building needs to begin from scratch.

If the majority of children have done Circle Time before then the chances are that a conducive environment for speaking and listening will be established fairly quickly. In our experience, repetition has not been a problem.

Circle Time focuses on the quality of the interaction between pupils and this will always provide new experiences and discussion points.

Speaking and Listening at Beginner Level

At this level pupils need to develop:

- awareness of others
- recognition and differentiation between sounds
- the ability to take turns to listen to people
- the ability to control impulse
- the ability to concentrate and remember what has been said
- to learning to interact positively with peers.

Pass Something On

Why?
- To establish turn-taking and the ability to wait for others to finish.
- To establish the basic structure of Circle Time.

Organisation:
- Whole group sitting in a circle.

Resources:
- An object to pass round.

How?
1. Ensure that pupils are quiet and attentive.
2. Explain that the object will be handed around the circle and that they should follow it with their eyes.
3. As it goes round ensure that no one's attention is wandering.
4. Give lots of praise.

Next Steps:
- Can they pass it round the other way?
- See how quickly they can do it. Time them?
- When someone whispers "change", the object changes direction and is passed round the other way.

Passing round a Word, Action, Touch or Smile

Why?
- To establish turn-taking and the ability to wait for others to finish.
- To establish the basic structure of Circle Time.

To begin to establish rapport.

Organisation:
Pupils sitting in a circle.

How?
1. Ensure that pupils are quiet and attentive.
2. Explain that a word, action, touch or smile will be handed round.
3. You begin by touching the person next to you on the shoulder, for example, and encourage them to pass it on.
4. Watch carefully. Pupil needs will become apparent as they try this simple task.

Things to pass on:
- a handshake
- a greeting gesture from the culture of a person in the class
- a smile
- a frown (can they do this without giggling?)
- the word "hello"
- greeting words from other languages
- actions, e.g. touching your nose.

Next Steps:
Greetings words could be extended to sentences. For example, "Hello, my name is ..." (Still at this stage said to the person next to them.)
Holding hands a squeeze can be passed around.
For other ideas to build on this see co-operative games section.

Using a Mascot or soft toy

Why?
To establish turn-taking and the ability to wait for others to finish.
To establish the basic structure of Circle Time.
To start language work using the support of a mascot.

Organisation:
Pupils sitting in a circle.

Resources:
A mascot.

How?
1. Ensure that pupils are quiet and attentive.

2. Explain that the mascot needs to be reminded of everyone's name.
3. Each pupil holds the mascot and tells it their name.

Extensions

Pupils can say name to the circle whilst holding the mascot

Pupils can give basic personal information whilst holding the mascot, for example, "My favourite food is ..."

The rules of Circle Time can be introduced (i.e. only the person holding the mascot allowed to speak, everyone listening kindly or with respect to that person).

Several different objects can be used to facilitate different speaking topics, for example;

- Sad cushion pad - passed round and held as pupils recall or talk about sad moments.
- Proud cloud - Pink and white cotton wool passed round as pupils recall proud moments.
- Love glove: Pupils talk of five things they love , one for each finger, as they pass the glove.
- Share chair: A model armchair to invoke discussion of who they would like to share a cosy chair with.
- Wish dish: a pretty dish which allows pupils to express three wishes.
- Power flower: artificial flower that grants power for one day. How would they use it?
- Able label: Pupils say what they are now able to do that they couldn't do (... a year ago. ... a term ago. ...last week. etc.)
- Laugh scarf: Bright scarf passed while pupils share ideas of what makes them laugh.
- Groan bone: A small bone (dog's toy perhaps) for pupils to air what makes them groan.

Source : Jeanne Holloway "Rainbow of Words."

Sentence completion

How?

1. Introduce a topic: What I had for breakfast, My family, Colours, Food, Games, whatever is topical.
2. Give pupils the beginning of a sentence to complete individually in a go-round.
3. Start with short sentences in the present tense e.g. "I like...........? (food, drink, colour, weather). "I enjoy..........." (game, school activity). "I can ...." (physical skill, curriculum activity). "I have..........." (parts of the

body, objects, numbers, things from a lucky dip bag).

4. Gradually introduce longer sentence beginnings and different tenses e.g. "My best game is...... My favourite dinner is..........Something I'm good at is........ In my family there is my............Today I am going to................ Someone who helped me this morning was.........................When I go shopping I like to...........Once when I was a baby I.......................When I'm old I'm going to...............If I could have a wish I would wish for............ "

Using Music

Why?
To establish turn-taking and the ability to wait for others to finish.
To establish the basic structure of Circle Time.
Links in with N.C. for Music.

Organisation
Pupils sitting in a circle.

Resources
Various musical instruments are needed.

How?
1. Ensure that pupils are quiet and attentive.
2. Start by passing round a single clap, then progress to an easy rhythm and, then a rhythm on an instrument around the circle.
3. Repeat using sounds made on musical instruments.

Extensions
Games could be introduced where pupils try:
To guess a song from its rhythm.
To pass a tambourine without making a sound (a good calming activity).
Guess what instrument was sounded by a classmate.
Children's traditional circle games often involve singing, (e.g. Ring of Roses, Blue Bell Windows, Farmer in his/her Den) and can be used to help them get used to working in a circle, hearing and remembering words and having fun together.

Asking questions

Why?
Practice at framing simple questions.
Fun.

<u>How?</u>
Sausage.
  1. One person sits in the middle.
  2. Everyone in the circle puts a question in turn to the person in the middle.
  3. To every question the person in the middle must answer "Sausage."
  The object is not to laugh
      Q. What's your favourite colour?
      A. Sausage.
      Q. What is our teachers name?
      A. Sausage.
  4. How many questions can they survive without laughing?
  5. How many different questions can the group think of to ask?

Source: Anna Scher & Charles Verrall (1984).

Listening

| ***Making a Silence*** |

<u>Why?</u>
  To extend the skills of listening.

<u>Organisation:</u>
  Pupils in a circle.

<u>How?</u>
  1. Pupils "make a silence". This could be a timed activity or could use different signals such as putting the speaking object used in Circle Time away in a box, miming closing shutters or drawing a curtain.
  2. There should be silence until the time is up, object is restored or curtains opened.
  3. Pupils are asked to sit comfortably in silence but to listen out for sounds outside the classroom.
  4. When the silence is over they can report what they heard.
      Pupils could listen for the sounds inside the room.
      Pupils could listen to their own thoughts and then report and respond.

<u>Extension: Listening and differentiating</u>
  Use the same technique to establish a silence.
  Turn listening into a game by having a number of objects, substances for people to make a sound with. Use small containers (stock cube boxes) filled in pairs with different things, to listen for matching sounds. (2 sand, 2 pebbles.)

Use percussion instruments and ask what the sound is doing..... getting louder, softer, faster, slower etc.

Listening and remembering

Remember what I like

Why?
   To encourage careful listening.
   To remember what has been said.
   To repeat accurately what has been said.

How?
   1. Class sits in a circle.
   2. Someone begins with the statement "My name is .... I like ...."
   3. Child to their right repeats "Your name is .... You like ....", "My name is .... I like.
   4. This continues around the circle, each child repeating statements and then adding their own.
   5. Game finishes with the teacher repeating everyone's statements.
   6. You could stick to themes e.g. food, games, TV programmes, or vary the statements "I am good at ...."

Circle whispers

Why?
   To encourage accurate listening and repeating of words or phrases.
   To carry out simple instructions.

Resources:
   A number of objects; anything to hand will do e.g. chalk, ruler, cup.

How?
   1. First try sending a whisper round the group.
   2. Next try sending an instruction (e.g. clap your hands) which the last person in the group carries out.
   3. Now give the group a selection of articles placed in the middle of the circle.
   4. This time the whisperer gives a short instruction for the last person to carry out with one or more of the articles e.g. put the chalk in the cup.
   5. Change the starting and ending persons so that everyone has a go.
   6. Keep a tally of how many times the whisper was right (younger children could thread a bead or stack a block, perhaps).

It takes a long time for a whisper to go all the way round the class, so this can be done in small groups if preferred. Instead of whispering, imaginary shapes or letters can be drawn with a finger on each others backs.

Speaking and Listening at Intermediate Level

Speaking and listening at intermediate level ideally builds on work done at beginner level. If, however, the ground rules of Circle Time haven't already been established, then it's important to do so from the start.

Pupils will need to develop:
- listening for understanding
- the ability to retain information and feed back to someone
- an understanding of what makes a good listener
- the ability to express thoughts and opinions.

As well as being appropriate for older primary pupils, the naming and mixing games and Intermediate speaking and listening activities, can form the basis of the first few weeks of personal and social education time for a year 7 or year 8 class. If this is done as a whole-school initiative other curriculum areas can then consolidate and build on these skills.

Go-Rounds

Why?
To establish a classroom culture of listening, trust and respect.
To develop pupil speaking skills.
To enable pupils to get to know each other better, and strengthen links between them.

Organisation:
Pupils sitting in a circle.

Resources:
A Circle Time object to be passed round.

How?
1. Ensure that class is quiet and attentive.
2. Remind them if necessary of the ground rules and ask them why they think they are important.
3. Explain subject of the go-round, e.g. "My favourite food is ...."
4. Ask who would like to begin. Pass them the speaking object. When they have had their turn they pass it to the person on their left or their right.

5. The object is passed clockwise or anti-clockwise around the circle with whoever is holding the object, including any adults sitting in the circle, having their turn to speak or saying "pass".

6. When everyone has had a go, the object is handed back to those who passed to give them another go.

Circle Time pairwork

Why?
> To develop pupils' ability to interact with every other person in the class.
> To strengthen links between pupils outside of their normal friendship groups and thus improve group cohesion.

Organisation:
> Pupils working in pairs whilst remaining in a circle.

Resources:
> A speaking object.

How?
1. Jumble the group up.
2. Pair the pupils off around the circle.
3. Give the pairs a subject, e.g. "Find out one thing you didn't already know about your partner." or "Find two things you both have in common." and then give them two minutes of discussion time.
4. Each pair reports back to the circle, e.g. "This is Amy, she looks after her grandad's pigeons." (Amy then reports on her partner). Or "What we both have in common is ....."
5. Loads of praise given to pairs who worked well together.

Extension:
Pairs and individuals can be given a range of sentences to complete in a go-round. For example:
> If I could make all the rules, I would ......
> If I had all the money in the world, I would ...
> My favourite place to be is ....
> In school/ after school what I like doing most of all is ......
> One thing I can do this year that I couldn't do last year is .....
> The best day I ever had was ...
> The most exciting thing that happened to me was .....
> One time I felt fed up was ....
> One thing I would like to do in life is .....
> We both like ......

We've both been to .....
We've both read .... and we think it's ....
We both think you could help other people by .....
We both think one thing to make school better would be .....
We both think a way of stopping accidents in the playground would be ....

Small group work

In small groups of five, pupils are given one each of one of the five senses (sight, sound, taste, touch, smell) as their topic. They tell the others in their group one thing they like and one thing they dislike to see, hear, taste, touch or smell. The groups then reform into groups of the same "sense" (e.g. all the sounds together) and report back to each other.

Listening checks

Why?
> To demonstrate that certain types of listening are active and not passive.
> To develop self esteem in pupils who feel listened to by the rest of the class.

Organisation:
> Pupils sitting in a circle.

Resources:
> An object to pass round.

How?
> 1. After a go-round send the talking object round the circle again. One person who has eyes closed suddenly says "Stop". The person holding the object at that moment stands up.
> 2. Ask who remembers what was the contribution made by the standing person.
> 3. Loads of praise for good listening.

Paired listening

Five questions

Why?
> To practise listening to and remembering information.

<u>Organisation:</u>
   Pairwork.

<u>How?</u>
   1. In this activity the pupils are given five questions that they are to ask their partner. The questions should be very simple, like;
      What is your favourite food?
      How do you get to school?
      Who lives in your family?
      What is your favourite T.V. programme?
      What do you hate?
   2. The pupils ask the questions one after another and try to remember what their partner said without taking notes.
   3. When each pupil has given five responses their partner tries to repeat back what they have heard. At the end the pupils give each other feedback about how accurately they were listening.

Thirty second pairwork

<u>Why?</u>
   To identify what makes a good listener.

<u>Organisation:</u>
   Pairwork.

<u>How?</u>
   1. The teacher times the pupils to work in twos, preferably sitting in a circle, to listen to each other for thirty seconds in a specific way.
   2. The first time both pupils are asked if they can keep talking simultaneously for thirty seconds without taking any notice of what the other is saying.
   3. The second time one of the pupils is told to speak whilst the other uses body language to suggest that they are bored or not interested in listening.
   4. The third time the same pupil who has not been heard has the opportunity of speaking again with their partner using body language to show that they are listening.

The discussion can focus on what each situation felt like and on what the body signals that we use to let people know that we are listening or not listening are. Finally make a list of "what makes a good listener" to include
        eye contact, facial expression, body language
        interest and acceptance

remembering what you said to them
not taking over by talking themselves.

Circle Stories

These activities encourage listening, inventiveness and quick thinking. Pupils sit in a circle.

| Sentence story |

How?
   1. Contribute one sentence each to develop a story round the circle.
   2. Each contribution should build on the sense of the last sentence

Extension:
   One word story made up from contributions of one word from each pupil round the circle

| Fortunately/unfortunately |

How?
   1. Pupils alternate by using sentences which begin with "Fortunately..." and "Unfortunately..."
   2. Contributions must be consistent with the meaning of the story and you could forbid simple opposites.

| Same story different endings |

Two or more pupils go out. The first one comes back in the room. Pupils start off a prearranged story and the pupil entering the room finishes it. The second person comes in and finishes the same story and so on.

Source: Anna Scher and Charles Verrall (1994).

| Just a minute |

Another good game is "Just a minute" which follows the rules of the radio quiz game of that name, where individuals have to talk for one minute on a given topic without deviating, repeating or hesitating. Other "contestants" can take over by saying "buzz" whenever they notice deviation, repetition or hesitation and can finish off the minute of talking. In the beginning try "Just half a minute".

Circle discussion

<u>Why?</u>
To practise listening, summarising and contributing to a topic.

<u>Organisation:</u>
Circle time using a speaking object.

<u>How?</u>
1. One person introduces a topic by reading a news item or summarising an issue of interest to everyone.
2. Give pupils a little time to discuss informally with a partner what their response to this is.
3. Open the discussion up to the circle, using Circle Time ground rules. Anyone who wants to contribute must take the speaking object, but before they make their point they must first summarise what the last person said.

Telephone a picture

<u>Why?</u>
To learn to give clear and accurate information.
To listen carefully and respond to information.
To learn to make adjustments.

<u>Organisation:</u>
First as a whole class activity, then in pairs or small groups.

<u>Resources :</u>
Materials for children to be able to duplicate pictures i.e. drawing materials, collage materials, paper, card, board, felt shapes. See page 51 for examples.

<u>How?</u>
1. As a practise, begin with a simple picture comprising 2 or 3 regular shapes. One person describes this picture to the class who have to draw or construct it without seeing it.
2. Discuss misunderstandings and difficulties and make a list of useful describing or directional words.
3. The activity can then be repeated in groups or pairs with whole-class or individual pictures transmitted.
4. One group of pupils could act as facilitators to the other groups or pairs. Pictures can be cascaded from individual to pairs, to fours etc. or sent down a line of pairs.
5. As pictures become more complex the vocabulary list needs expanding.

Asking Questions

<u>Why?</u>
To practise formulating simple questions.
To introduce pupils to closed questions (YES/NO answers).

<u>Organisation:</u>
Pupils in a circle.

<u>How?</u>
1. One person in the middle.
2. Everyone in turn puts one question to the person in the middle which has a yes or no answer.
3. The person in the middle must answer the opposite of the truth:
    Q. Are you a Sea Lion?
    A. Yes
    Q. Did you have Sea Weed for breakfast?
    A. Yes
    Q. Have you got two ears?
    A. No.

Source: Anna Scher and Charles Verrall (1984).

<u>Extension:</u>
Television or chat show host interviewing guest.

How to Hold a Conversation

<u>Why?</u>
To practise using open-ended questions.
To begin to develop rapport.

<u>Organisation:</u>
Pair work and role play.

<u>How?</u>
1. Characters: Half the pupils decide on a character they will all role play, and something which has happened to the character which they feel very strongly about:
    • a football manager who has just been sacked
    • a dancer who has just broken a leg
    • an old person who has just won the lottery
    • a person who has just had a first baby.
2. Questioners: The other half decide on a range of questions they might ask

someone they were meeting for the first time.

3. Each character is then paired off with a questioner who tries to find out who they are and what has happened to them.
4. Feed back to the whole group on successes in gaining information.
5. Whole group list examples of questions: "What's on your mind?" or phrases "Tell me more about that." which help people to give plenty of information.
6. Characters and questioners swop parts to role play in pairs a situation such as:
    - entertaining a guest from Mars
    - meeting a new neighbour
    - spending break - time with someone famous.
7. In the circle feedback what they did well and whole group pool ideas on what puts people at their ease
what helps conversation to flow.

Extension:
Listen to radio interview or watch T.V. chat show interview and list kinds of questions which helped people to talk a lot. Using a tape recording or video would make a more permanent record of this activity.

Speaking and Listening at Advanced Level

Young people who have developed competency and confidence in using the speaking and listening skills practised so far can progress to using reflective listening, clarifying and summarising to support each other in reviewing progress, evaluating work and identifying action points.

The nature of group discussion and pairwork will reflect issues of concern to them and may even include a formal agenda board of items of their choosing. (See the Problem Solving and Conflict Resolution chapter for ways of facilitating this process.)

If the conventions of Circle Time are established early in a school, then this will pay dividends across a variety of curriculum areas, not just in the more obvious areas of English and Drama. The National Oracy Project's booklet published through the National Curriculum Council Teaching, "Talking and Learning in Key Stage Three", stresses the importance of talk for learning and summarises the ways in which the National Curriculum draws upon talk across the curriculum. All of these uses, activities and contexts lend themselves to the process of Circle Time, and further reinforce the importance of group collaboration and the identity of the individual as a respected and necessary member of the group.

Uses:

- expressing feelings and opinions about themselves, a subject or activity
- taking part in group discussions
- presenting ideas, information, texts
- interpreting arguments and developing them
- discriminating between fact and opinion
- summarising views to gain a consensus
- instructing and responding to instructions
- conveying information
- role play
- reflecting upon their own talk and learning the talk of others
- exploratory talk (predicting, speculating, hypothesising)
- demonstrating knowledge of language.

Activities:

- preparing presentations to class/school/parents
- planning and designing tasks, and setting and solving problems within them
- identifying specific outcomes for their own work
- making and testing hypotheses
- reporting and discussing stories, poems, plays and other texts
- reasoning and arguing
- using talk in shared reading or writing activity
- simulations and group drama, discussing and analysing language in use.

Contexts:

- across curriculum areas, e.g. the science laboratory, the technology room
- in a variety of groupings (paired, single-sex, small-group, class, with/without presence of teacher)
- in contact with audiences beyond the classroom
- in representative roles, acting on behalf of others
- using audio/video, radio, television, telephone, computer
- in enquiry and survey work in the locality or on field visits/trips
- in mini-enterprise, work shadowing or industry liaison exercise.

Clearly, a class of pupils who are used to respecting each other's right to speak and to be listened to, who are confident at speaking in front of each other, and who are used to the concept that everyone makes a contribution to class discussions, will be better placed than most to access those aspects of the National Curriculum that require pupils to use their speaking and listening skills.

Why?

> To stimulate creative thinking.
>
> To enable all pupils to give ideas, plan or give feedback on a particular area of work.
>
> To consolidate work done.
>
> To enable reflection on learning.

Organisation:

> Pupils sitting in a circle.

Resources:

> Talking object if desired.

How?

> 1. Get pupils into circle.
> 2. Use standard "go-round":
>   - to ascertain what the pupils remember of work done so far
>   - to brainstorm new ideas
>   - to plan the tasks that smaller groups will carry out
>   - for individuals, pairs or small groups to feed back how they are getting on with a task, or what they have done
>   - for pupils to give each other ideas, advice or feedback
>   - for pupils to summarise, consolidate or draw together the learning points in a particular area of work
>   - to evaluate work.

Curriculum-based pairwork and small group work

These activities are planned to:

- develop pupils' abilities to interact in a positive way with other pupils in the class
- help pupils to formulate, express and clarify their ideas through talk.

Pupils work in pairs and small groups, sometimes feeding back to a larger group.

Rainbow groups

A way of ensuring that pupils experience working alongside a range of others is to give each young person in a group a number, or a colour. When the group has worked together, all the pupils of the same number or colour form new groups to compare what they have done.

Envoys

Often, in group work, the teacher is concerned that she will be under pressure from many different directions. Envoying helps pupils to find help and support without necessarily having recourse to the teacher. If a group needs to check something, or to obtain information, one of the group can be sent as an "envoy" to the library, or book corner, or another group, and will then report back. Another use is to ask groups to send an envoy to a different group to explain what they have done, obtain responses and suggestions, and bring them back to the group.

Critical Friends

A group member is responsible for observing the ways in which the group works together. Using a simple guide list (which pupils can devise), the observer watches and listens as the students work. This information is then discussed by the group. This helps young people to develop their own evaluative strategies.

Listening - S.A.R.A.H.

Using the routine:

S top talking.
A ctive listening.
R epeat back what was said.
A ccept other's feelings.
H elp other to list some choices.

Why?
  To develop reflective listening skills.

Organisation:
  Circle Time, pairwork, groupwork.

Resources:
  Blackboard or flipchart.

How?
  1. In pairs give examples of different things you make a point of listening to, (news report, radio interview, friend with a problem, details of homework assignment).
  2. Brainstorm reasons for listening to the listed things (for information, to be entertained, as background noise etc.).
  3. Go-round. What makes the difference in the way we listen? Suppose one

example was of a radio commentary of a cricket match and the other was a friend or relative with a problem.....Teacher or pupil to summarise the go-round.

4. Recap what makes a good listener (intermediate speaking and listening) and what is "active" or requires effort in listening well.

5. In pairs take it in turns to tell each other of a time you experienced a problem with a piece of school work or between friends. The one not talking should try and listen well.

6. Feedback one thing my listener did well. One thing that would improve my feeling of being listened to.

7. Teacher gives the formula S.A.R.A.H.
   Stop talking.
   Active listening.
   Repeat back what has been said to you.
   Accept how the person is feeling and their view of things.
   Help them to list some choices about what to do.

8. In 3's pupils choose a speaker, a listener and an observer. The speaker chooses their own topic to talk about. The listener concentrates on using the SARAH technique. The observer watches the interaction ready to feedback what the listener did well and what they recommend might make it even better. The observer also keeps a check on the time limit of 3 minutes or whatever has been agreed.

9. The triads swop roles until all three have had a chance to try listening.

10. Final go-round focuses on what it felt like to be listened to so well and any other comments about how well the listener listened, observer feed-back etc.

Extension:
   Once pupils are practised at using reflective listening in Triads in this way, they can use this arrangement to review how they are getting on with project work or course work. Reflective listening is an important skill used in peer mediation, peer mentoring and other peer support processes. (See the Mediation chapter for further work.)

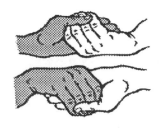

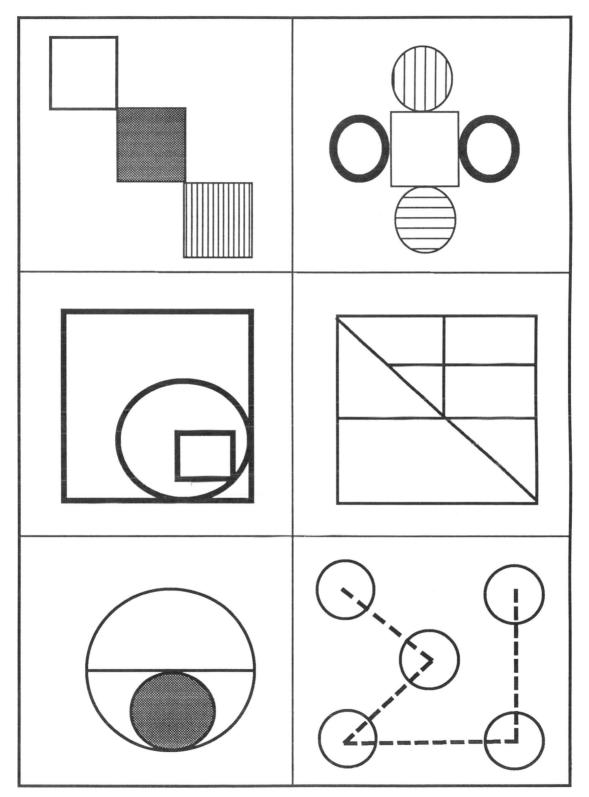

Chapter 5
Affirmation

Self esteem is the corner stone of this work. Many of the difficulties which teachers and pupils face in the classroom are linked to poor self-esteem. Raising pupil self esteem results in:

- reduced anxiety
- assertiveness
- reduced aggression
- improved relationships
- confidence
- willingness to try things out and to learn from mistakes
- reduced disruption
- raised standards of achievement.

As a training exercise, try asking half your staff to list the characteristics of a child with high self esteem and the other half to list the characteristics of a child who is achieving their potential. We are confident that the two lists will be interchangeable.

Raising self esteem can be justified on both personal, social and academic grounds. Clearly all children need to be told that they are special (some are never given that message at home) but they also need to have high and realistic expectations of themselves.

Adults and children will achieve up to a ceiling of their belief in their ability to achieve. If we can raise the ceiling of their belief in their own ability, we can raise their level of achievement. This has been shown through several pieces of research in the sixties, seventies and eighties.

Lawrence (1973) offered some brief training to volunteers and they then "counselled" groups of primary children identified as under achieving readers.
The results showed that the counselling had more effect on reading progress than extra teaching. Hartley (1986) demonstrates that children can significantly improve their performance when they attempt tasks in the role of the cleverest pupil in the class, and Clark and Walberg (1968) show that a group of ten to thirteen year old pupils who were praised frequently over three weeks showed a significantly greater improvement in reading attainment than a control group.

It can often be useful to connect a programme to raise self-esteem with raising standards. Improved pupil self-esteem will both reduce conflict and give young people the necessary confidence to work through their problems. It is an essential part of all peer mediation work.

Teacher Affirmation

There is growing recognition of the need to affirm children, The need for teachers to feel affirmed is often ignored. In the political climate of the nineties it is important for teachers to hold onto their self esteem and belief in their professional judgment. Don't underestimate the importance of building teacher self-esteem, including your own!

Many whole-school initiatives to raise pupil self-esteem fall down because teachers trying to be more positive towards children don't feel valued themselves. Empty vessels have nothing to give!

A series of teacher affirmations brainstormed by a group of Birmingham teachers:

√ You trained for a minimum of three years to do this job – believe in your judgment.

√ Parents and friends sometimes come and go, but teachers are there
√ every morning.

√ Notice how many tasks you completed this morning BEFORE even getting down to teaching!

√ Notice how many decisions you have made today.

√ Recognise that pupils have benefited from working with you today.

√ Acknowledge the new things that you have undertaken and learnt this week.

√ Notice the range of feelings you have intuitively responded to today.

√ Notice the range of learning needs you have tried to provide for today.

√ Notice how many different roles you have undertaken today.

√ Acknowledge each new awareness in yourself as a strength.

√ Public speaking, managing complex group dynamics, presentation and display, needs analysis, marketing, motivating the work force, financial management and administration, public relations..... all in one day!

Beginner Affirmation

At beginner level and for younger children, affirmation will often be centred around the warmth and affirming manner of the teacher, which will serve to create an atmosphere in which the pupils feel able to contribute. Eye contact, "well done", applause and even kneeling down next to children can all help to give them the support and confidence to participate in Circle Time.

Once an affirming and supportive atmosphere has been established, pupils can begin recognising their own, and other people's, strengths. Vocabulary is a priority at all levels of affirmation work. People have lots of words to use as "put downs", but not so many in regular use as compliments and acknowledgments!

At beginner level the vocabulary of affirmation will clearly be different according to the age of the children. With 4 to 7 year olds a limited range of words may be chosen and these might concern newly acquired skills, or physical characteristics, rather than more abstract qualities. With junior and lower secondary pupils the range of vocabulary may be increased and pupils will be encourage to consider qualities from across a wide range of categories. At upper secondary level affirmation work will tend to be more reflective, summative and evaluative and would fit in well with records of achievement.

The difficulty of publicly stating something that we are good at should not be underestimated, and at beginner level this should not be expected of pupils.

At this level pupils need to develop:

- a wider vocabulary of affirmation
- the ability to recognise their own strengths and those of their peers, in limited non-threatening ways.

Most special person

This is a lovely activity, which uses discovery to make a very important point. It can really only be used once, except where it has been used in early years education and repeated much later on at top junior or lower secondary level.

Why?
To make the point that each person is unique and special.
To begin to reflect on and identify positive qualities and skills.

Resources:
   A safety mirror and box to contain it.

How?
   1. Begin by identifying people the group think are really special and ask pupils to say what it is that makes them so special.
   2. Tell pupils that you have a picture in a box of the most special person in the whole class. You are going to let them see who that is, but they must not say anything until everyone has seen who the person is. (This is an important test of impulse control. You could begin by discussing what to do if you feel yourself wanting to shout out or say something. You could also offer it as a challenge with a reward if everyone manages it.)
   3. Pass round the box with the mirror inside so that pupils can see that the most special person in the whole class is them. (Don't forget to look in there yourself!)
   4. Celebrate having managed the challenge and reinforce the point that every individual is important and special in your group.

Extensions:
   Go on to help pupils to identify for each other what makes them special.
   Make it a policy to include examples of every child's work for display.
   Take photographs of the whole class or tutor group and display them with positive comments.
   Play games to mix and integrate pupils and to make sure that they know and use each other's names. (see Name games and Mixing games section.)

Up downs

Why?
   To celebrate diversity and accept differences.
   To learn more about each other.
   To publicly affirm each other.

Organisation:
   Sitting in a circle.

How?
   1. Begin with everyone sitting down.
   2. When a category is mentioned which applies to them, pupils stand up.
   3. Those who remain seated give a round of applause to those who are standing.
   4. After the applause pupils sit down again. This is meant to be a fairly quick activity.

5. Use a variety of different categories which help pupils to acknowledge each other, making sure that every characteristic is included.

"If you have.......brown hair, black hair, blonde hair, long, short, curly, straight etc."
"If you are the ...youngest /oldest / in the middle / an only child in your family."
"If you celebrate...Eid / Diwali / Hanukah / Xmas / Chinese New Year etc."
"If you can speak two / three / four / languages."

Positive adjectives

Why?
To increase vocabulary of affirmation.

Organisation:
Brainstorming.

Resources:
Flip chart or large piece of paper and pens.

How?
i) Beginner 4 to 7 year olds.
1. Ask them to tell you kind words to describe children. You might want to list this under activities e.g. "She helps me (helpful) ". "She plays with me (friendly) " and skills e.g. "She can tie her laces" "He can find his coat peg" "She can run fast" etc.
2. Find some way of recording the words that is appropriate to the age and abilities of the children.

ii) Beginner Junior and Secondary pupils.
1. Ask them to brainstorm in small groups positive qualities and skills which they admire or appreciate on other people across the following categories:
   √ personal strengths
   √ practical abilities
   √ sports abilities
   √ artistic abilities
   √ intellectual abilities
   √ social strengths
   √ emotional strengths.
2. Get the groups to feed back to the whole group and write up the ideas.
3. Create a more permanent display to be put up where it can be referred to during later affirmation work.

Affirmation Prompts

The following list that we have prepared could be used to prompt a wider range of ideas and to offer something for pupils to choose words and phrases to apply to themselves and each other.

Personal qualities
"Funny" is not included to encourage pupils to think of other words to express good humour or wit. "Nice" is not included either.

adventurous	amiable	attractive
ambitious	assertive	bright
bubbly	brave	calm
compassionate	caring	considerate
courteous	courageous	cheerful
determined	diplomatic	dynamic
efficient	encouraging	energetic
enterprising	expressive	exciting
fair	friendly	generous
gentle	giving	happy
helpful	honest	humorous
independent	interesting	kind
loving	optimistic	patient
pleasant	positive	persistent
reliable	resourceful	responsible
risk-taking	self respecting	sensible
special	spontaneous	sympathetic
trustworthy	vivacious	witty

Practical abilities
- make or repair things well
- good model maker
- organise belongings
- help with housework
- keep school papers and books tidy
- help with shopping
- help to keep classroom tidy
- wash the car
- look after younger children and babies
- have a hobby or special activity
- look good by taking a pride in my appearance

- know how to cook something or how to wash-up
- keep my things in good condition
- mend my bike or skate board
- make my bed
- wash and dress myself
- make my own packed lunch.

Sports abilities

- keep myself fit
- have a special skill in one sport
- am a good team member
- have tried something new
- have really persevered in order to be able to do something
- am getting braver at doing something in P.E. or sports
- can keep to the rules of a game
- am a good loser.

Artistic abilities

- have a special skill in music, dance, painting, drawing, pottery, writing stories, writing poems, colouring in, designing machines or clothes, arranging objects, plants or flowers so that they look beautiful
- can design and make a model
- am good at acting out stories
- am getting better at something
- have tried hard to produce a good picture or story.

Intellectual abilities

- can solve problems
- am curious to discover new things
- understand things quickly...like films, TV programmes, books and information
- keep trying until I get things right
- think things through before I act or make a decision
- can talk easily to other children and adults
- am getting better at writing clearly
- am skilled with numbers, on paper, in my head
- can concentrate well
- know how things work
- can understand diagrams and graphs
- am intuitive about other people's feelings

- am good at working out why people do things
- am good at learning from mistakes
- can see patterns and repetitions
- can use tools and equipment well
- can use technology.

Social strengths

- help other people in my class
- look after people younger than me
- join in playing
- ask people who are feeling left out or sad to join in
- notice when people are not feeling happy
- try to be a good friend
- try to speak kindly to everyone
- get on well with members of my class
- am interested in other people
- listen to other people
- try to see things from other people's point of view
- am reliable
- keep arrangements or agreements made with others
- am getting better at getting on with people
- am getting better at keeping my temper
- can stay calm and friendly when people have a different point of view
- treat other people with respect
- am good at helping two people who have fallen out to sort their problem out
- have a good sense of humour
- can laugh with other people instead of laughing at them
- am good at remembering to say thank you or well done to people.

Emotional strengths

- can recognise how I am feeling
- can guess how others are feeling
- can stay calm when I need to
- can appear confident when I need to, even when I don't feel sure of myself
- know how and when to let off steam safely
- can ask for support when I need it

- know when it is time to withdraw from a situation
- know when to stand up for my rights
- can express my anger safely
- can wait for things, even when i want them badly
- know how to respond when someone is upset or angry
- can cry when I need to
- can see the funny side of things.

Mr. U'Glee

Why?
    To demonstrate negative effects of name-calling and positive effects of
    affirmation.

Organisation:
    Pupils working in whole group.

Resources:
    Blackboard and chalk.

How?
    1. Draw an ugly "Mr. U'Glee" on the board.
    2. Ask the pupils to shout out words to describe him.
    3. With every negative comment, rub a bit out and with every positive com-
    ment draw a bit in.
    4. At the end, discuss how saying horrible things about people makes them
    "disappear."

Source: Adapted from Ulster QPE Project.

Class challenge

Why?
    To reward those pupils who are able to refrain from making negative com-
    ments.
    To show this as a positive skill.
    To set a short-term target for those pupil who find it difficult to refrain from
    making negative comments.

Resources:
    A class list pinned to the wall and some gold stars.

<u>Organisation:</u>
Pupils working in whole group.

<u>How?</u>
1. You set the class a challenge. How many of them can get through a morning (a day, an hour) without saying anything nasty to anyone?
2. At the end of the time period set, the teacher asks who has achieved this goal. There may be some discussion about this.
3. Pupils who have earned it receive a star next to their name.

<u>Extensions:</u>
Include badges and awards for people who behave with respect towards each other.
Lorry drivers used to have a "Knight of the Road" award for courteous driving.
Pupils could design their own awards to denote courtesy, careful use of equipment, consideration, etc.

Intermediate Affirmation

At this level pupils can draw on a vocabulary generated at beginner level to affirm themselves and others in ways that feel safe for them.

At junior and lower secondary level affirmation is often about countering a culture of name-calling, put downs and bullying which can take the form of "cussing" and swearing against each other's families.

This developmental stage (8 to 12 year olds, Kohlberg 1987) involves them giving an increased importance to relationships with their peers, and testing out more sophisticated social skills. This can often mean power struggles, the formation of cliques and sub-groups, the isolation of children who don't fit in and intense friendships that blow hot and cold.

Affirmation work can support all pupils in retaining their self-esteem as a valued member of the class, and can educate children who are demonstrating some of these behaviours into more positive behaviour patterns.

At this level pupils of all ages need to develop:
• the ability to identify or accept, a personal quality, strength or skill and tell a partner
• the ability to feedback a partner's personal quality or strength, on their behalf, to the whole group
• the confidence to produce a display of qualities within the class

- the ability to affirm other members in a small group and receive either verbal or written affirmation
- an awareness of how hurtful it is to laugh at or contradict the self affirmation of others.

Affirmation pairwork

Why?
> To enable pupils who might find it hard to say a personal quality or strength to the whole class to say it to a partner.
> To enable pupils to hear someone else saying what makes them special publicly.

Organisation:
> Circle Time pairwork.

How?
> 1. Use the pairwork structure to get pupils to choose a positive adjective to describe themselves that begins with the same letter as their name. e.g. Dynamic Davinder, Serene Simon. After the partner has fed back, "This is amiable Andrew" the whole class repeat together the adjective and name.

> 2. Help pupils to make their own private "I can..........." list or series of pictures. This will be good preparation for the next activity.

> 3. Use the Circle Time pairwork structure to identify and feedback on behalf of your partner some or all of these (spread over a series of sessions). Choose carefully and ensure that no negative comments slip in.

> One thing:
> - that (name) is good at........
> - that makes him/her special.........
> - that he/she is doing his/her best in...........
> - that is pleased with................
> - that (name) has achieved against the odds ....
> - that not many people know about (name) is....................
> - If (name) were a car/animal/building he/she would be ....because...........................

Car wash

Why?
> To generate good feelings and group cohesion.
> To encourage positive touching.

62

To consolidate "nice words".

Organisation:
Pupils stand in two lines facing each other like the two sides of a car wash.

How?
1. One volunteer pupil has a turn at being a "car", starting in the middle at one end of the two lines.
2. The pupil walks through the "car wash" and receives pats on the back, applause, nice words and cheers.

Source: Murray White (1991).

Thank-you cards

Why?
To encourage pupils to appreciate what other people do for them, and what skills others have.

Organisation:
Pupils working in whole group.

How?
1. Talk about people who help us.
2. Discuss how they help.
3. What makes them good at what they do?
4. Each pupil designs and produces a "thank-you" card for someone who helps them at school or at home.
5. Write why they are saying thank you.
6. Share end results with the rest of the class.
7. Could some of the recipients come in to tell the class how they felt when they received the card?

Letter writing

Why?
To enable contact with pupils in other schools.
To give a real audience for affirmation work.

Organisation:
Pupils working individually.

Paper, pencils, envelopes and the address of a school which has agreed to join in this activity.

How?
1. Find a class in another school, in England or abroad, to pair up with.
2. Encourage the pupils to write a letter to another pupil, stating a bit about themselves, especially what they are good at and/or proud of.
3. Get them to ask questions about the letter recipient which will encourage him or her to reply in similar terms.

Fruit bowl

Why?
To create a class display of strengths.

Organisation:
Pupils working in whole group.

Resources:
A large display background picture of an empty fruit bowl.
One sheet of card or sugar paper, fruit shape, for each member of the class.
Glue. Pens and pencils.

How?
1. Each pupil cuts out and writes onto their piece of fruit one thing that makes them special.
2. The fruit is stuck onto the fruit bowl.
3. The teacher and class discuss how our strengths and gifts to each other are different but complimentary like the fruit in a fruit bowl.

Source: The Kingston Friends Workshop Group.

Extensions:
Other ideas for class or whole school displays include:

an affirmation tree in the assembly hall where an achievement for each and every pupil is written onto a leaf which is attached to a branch of a large "tree"

pupils write affirmations onto large foot prints which they stick on top of the insults that they never want to hear again

pupils write strengths onto stars or candles that are put up as a display

pupils write the gifts which they bring to the class e.g. humour, friendship etc. onto a paper link that becomes part of a class paper chain, or the ribbon tying individual parcels.

Advanced Affirmation

At this level pupils need to develop:
- the ability to say publicly what they are good at / proud of
- the ability to receive affirmation
- the ability to reflect on their achievements and strengths as part of putting together their record of achievement
- the ability to be consistently accepting of others self affirmation.

Affirmation go-rounds

Why?

To help pupils to be clear about their personal strengths and those of others.

Organisation:

Pupils sitting in a circle.

Resources:

A list of positive qualities in people displayed somewhere in the room.

How?

Use the go-round structure to complete the sentences:
- One thing I do well is ....
- I'm skilled at...........
- A positive thing about me is........
- Something you can rely on me for is.............
- My ambition is.............
- My friends like me because .....

Fame for the day

Why?

To improve self-esteem.
To encourage pupils to appreciate each other's good points.

Organisation:

Pupils working in whole group.

Resources:

Paper and pen for a scribe or the teacher.

How?

1. A pupil is chosen at random to have fame for the day, no particular reasons is necessary. (Pupils need to know that all will eventually have their turn.)
2. He/she is treated as a special person for the day.
3. When the pupil is first chosen the rest of the class brainstorm the things that they like about that pupil.
4. This can be written up later and presented as a certificate for the pupil to take home.

Affirming each other

Why?

To develop skills from recognising personal strengths to making public things that you appreciate about others.

To be able to make eye contact and say directly to someone what it is that you appreciate about them.

Organisation :

Pupils sitting in a circle or in small groups of five or six.

Resources:

An appropriate object to pass round.

How?

1. In the whole class group this can be simply a spontaneous opportunity to express thanks or appreciation of each other. With small groups every pupil will need to receive the object at least once.
2. Invite pupils to hand the object to others in the circle in recognition of support received or as a way of saying thank you for things that they have done.
3. As they hand the object to the person they say why. Encourage them to make eye contact with the person and to talk directly to them saying "I appreciate....." "I want to thank you for...." "I admire you for....." "It meant a lot to me when......"

Extensions:

Use a ball of string or wool instead of an object. As a compliment or thank you is given, the string is handed over so that it weaves backwards and forwards across the circle making a friendship web.

Lighthouse activity

Why?
To produce a written record of positive comments from peers.

Organisation:
Pupils sitting in a large circle or several smaller circles depending on how they will work best.

Resources:
A lighthouse sheet (see page 69) for everyone.
A pencil per pupil.
A clipboard per pupil

How?
1. Pupils write their names on their sheet.
2. They pass their sheet to their left.
3. They write a positive comment on the Lighthouse that has been passed to them about the pupil whose name is on the sheet.
4. Facilitator circulates to be certain that no negative comments are written on anyone's Lighthouse. Comments such as "funny" and "Don't know" can be hurtful. (If there is a real likelihood of negative comments from pupils this activity should not be attempted.)
5. Pupils keep passing sheets to their left and writing positive comments until their own returns to them.
6. Pupils read their sheets and maybe feedback which comments they particularly liked.

Extensions:
This can be done by sticking a piece of paper to people's backs, onto which positive comments are written by others as they circulate.
(See Cooperation Chapter for Peer Appraisal.)

How name-calling hurts us

Why?
To raise the pupil's awareness of the damaging effects of name-calling.
To enable them to develop their own strategies for reducing it.

Resources:
The name-calling sheet from page 70.

Organisation:
Pupils working individually.

How?
1. Decide what you would like to do about confidentiality. Do you want them to put their names on the sheets?
2. Give out the sheets and ask the pupils to write privately onto them.
3. Take them in and read them.
4. On another occasion - use Circle Time to read some of the findings and comments without identifying anyone.
5. Give them the talking object and invite them to use their Circle Time to say whatever they need to about the name-calling that is going on.
6. The pupils could make pledges to reduce name-calling.
7. Pledges could form the basis of a classroom contract on name-calling, or they could write a pledge on a piece of paper and put it in an envelope to be reviewed at the end of term.

Extension:
See "Understanding Conflict" in the Problem Solving chapter.

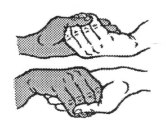

Lighthouse

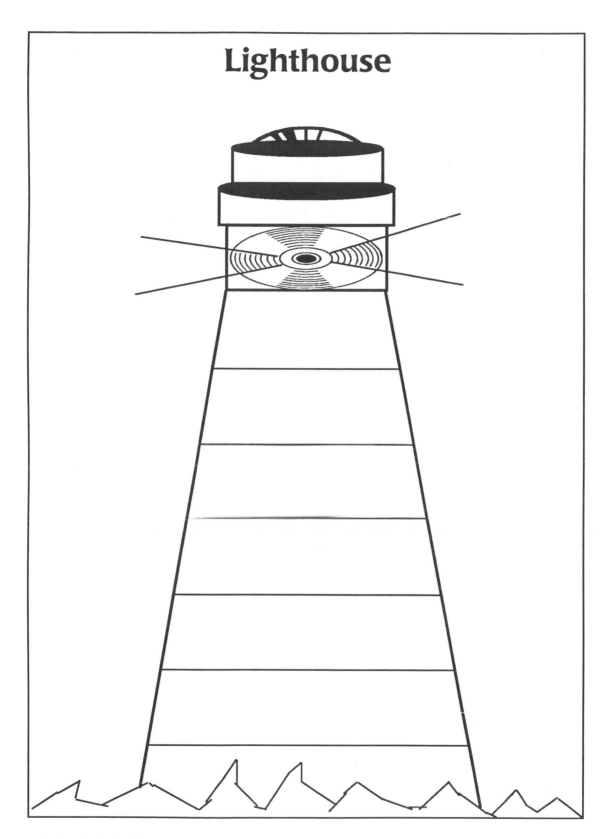

Name Calling

Name: [   ]

1. How often do people call you names? Circle your answer.

   never / not very often / quite a lot / all the time

2. What sort of things do they say ?

3. Do you call people names? How often?

   If so, then what sort of names?

4. How do you feel inside when someone calls you a name?

5. How do you feel inside when you have called someone else a name?

6. On the other side of this sheet, write about a time when you remember someone calling you a name. How did it make you feel? What did you do?

Chapter 6
Cooperation

The mediation process revolves around cooperation. Much of the foundation work for this is teaching the value of cooperation and the not inconsiderable skills involved.

Cooperation in the classroom has three elements;
- pairwork
- small groupwork
- whole group work.

All three are important and require slightly different skills. The third element is particularly important for developing class cohesion and for countering the effect of sub-groups, cliques and gender or ethnicity divides. Circle Time is a powerful tool in this context.

The need to teach cooperation skills is strong.

The idea that two people experiencing conflict can come to a solution where they are both winners (a win-win solution) is central to re-educating young people who believe that there is only one right answer to difficulties or problems and that only the strongest and toughest will survive.

Aronson, E., Bridgeman, D. L. and Geffner, R. (1978) have evaluated the jigsaw approach to co-operative learning (each small group of children is assigned a segment of a lesson and the groups must co-operate in order to get the full picture) and have shown that compared with the controls, the children in the jigsaw learning groups were more helpful, considerate of others, and co-operative. They also expressed greater self-esteem and increased liking for other children of their own and other ethnic groups, as well as more positive attitudes towards school and learning.

Teacher Cooperation

Some questions to consider:
- Do the staff in your school work together cooperatively?
- Is everyone's contribution to schemes of work and lesson plans pooled together?
- Are staff members open and sharing, willing to support each other?
- Do you know what part the work you are doing with your year group plays in the overall school development plan?

- How are decisions made in your school?
- In what ways do you cooperate with other schools to ensure smooth transition from phase to phase?
- Are you in competition with other schools in your area or does co-operation mean more for all of you?
- Are you part of a consortium of schools pooling expertise and resources effectively for the benefit of all?

Beginner Cooperation

A number of nursery and infant teachers have expressed to us their concern about the aggressive nature of play amongst some pre-school and infant children. Supporting cooperative play provides essential practise for later cooperative styles of learning. Very young children are still developing a sense of self and will progress towards cooperation through reciprocal relationships, learning to share, to take turns and to contribute to activities of all kinds.

People of all ages will benefit from starting with these beginner activities.

Parachute games

Why?
To show that some things can only be achieved by working together.

Organisation:
The whole class working together in a large enough space.

Resources:
A parachute.

How?
1. Explain why you are playing with the parachute.
2. Begin by all sitting around the edge of the spread out parachute holding onto the edge of it.
3. Play a variety of games including:

The Sea

Can they:
- flap the parachute up and down to make a quiet and then a stormy sea?
- make one wave go from one side of the parachute to the other?
- make a wave circle around the edge of the parachute?

Walking on the Sea

Can one person walk across the parachute whilst the others make a gentle wave?

Cat and Mouse

The cat walks (no shoes) on top of the parachute, the mouse crawls round underneath.

People holding the edge of the parachute wave it like the sea to disguise the bump that is the mouse underneath as it tries to get from one side of the parachute to the other without the cat finding it and touching it.

Sharks

People sit with their legs under the parachute. One person (the shark) crawls underneath and touches the feet of 5 other people who "disappear" underneath too.

Extensions:

When they can play these seated games well the pupils can then play other games standing up, including:

Dome

The children, all holding part of the parachute, raise their arms above their heads quickly and then lower them slowly, making a dome.

Swap places

Begin as in the Dome activity and whilst the parachute is making a Dome some children swap places before it falls again. Criteria for changing places can be ..colours of clothes, eyes, hair etc. pets, brothers and sisters, favourite books, toys, food or simply having your name called.

Ball and parachute

All holding the parachute, place a large ball on one side and ask people to help the ball to roll all the way round the circle without missing anyone out.

Place the ball in the middle, toss it into the air and catch it again.

Depending on the gap at the centre of your parachute and the size of ball used, ask people to roll the ball so that it goes down through the gap in the middle or so that it rolls to rest there.

Pass it on

Why?
To engage the whole class in an activity that is fun.

Organisation:
The whole class sitting or standing in a circle.

Resources :
A large loop of string big enough for everyone in the class to hold onto, with a ring or small block threaded onto it before the ends are tied.

How?
1. One person looks away whilst the others put their hands onto the string with one of them hiding the ring or block in their hand.
2. The person who looked away now guesses who is holding it whilst the ring is passed around the circle. People in the circle try to disguise who is passing the ring on by moving their hands together and apart.

Sharks 2

Why?
To encourage teamwork and friendly touching.

Organisation:
Children in a large space free to move around.

Resources:
About ten P.E. hoops on the floor spread around the space.

How?
1. Put the hoops on the floor spread around the place.
2. Pupils "swim" in the "sea" around the hoops or "islands".
3. When someone shouts "SHARKS" they get onto one of the islands, then at the "all clear" signal they start swimming outside again.
4. One by one you take the hoops away. When there are only a few left can they help each other to stay on the islands without dipping a foot into the sea?

Rainforest

<u>Why?</u>
To enable the creation of a whole group sound picture.
To encourage pupils to take their lead from one another, not the teacher.

<u>Organisation:</u>
Circle Time.

<u>How?</u>
1. Begin by passing a simple action or touch round the circle so that pupils can practice taking their cue from the person sitting next to them and not from across the circle or from the person leading the actions (at first this will be the adult).
2. Explain that you are going to use the sounds made from the actions that you are passing round the circle to build up a sound picture of a tropical rainstorm building up and dying away.
3. Remind them to copy the person next to them on their right (check they know right from left) and not to change what they are doing until that person changes.
4. Start by rubbing your hands together in a circular movement. The person on your right should do the same, followed by the person on their right and so on round the circle.
5. Next tap two fingers on your palm slowly. The person on your right then changes from rubbing hands to tapping fingers and so on round the circle.
6. When everyone is tapping their palm you start the next sound which is clapping an uneven rhythm like rain falling.
7. Thunder is next, made by stamping feet whilst still clapping.
8. The thunder of feet stops but clapping continues.
9. Clapping becomes palm tapping again.
10. Palm tapping becomes rubbing hands.
11. Rubbing hands then stops gradually round the circle as hands are placed on knees.
12. Silence.

People can then take the opportunity to notice what they all did well during this activity and to make suggestions about ways of making it even better.

<u>Extensions:</u>
This activity can be used to develop stories where the pupils in the circle create the accompanying sound pattern or the movements of the characters. (A centipede or caterpillar character provides a good start!)
Whole group work can then be extended into music making with percussion instruments and also into circle dancing.

Story telling can become drama work with groups of children choosing to be the same character. At first you may choose to do this as a static activity, with teacher narrating and pupils accompanying when their part in the story comes. Later pupils will enjoy the opportunity to play out the story with the narration and accompanying sound track provided for them by percussion instruments.

Family or tribe casting

A group of the same characters. (When pupils are ready, this can provide early practice of leadership if an activity is included for a family leader.)

Conglomerate casting

Several pupils building themselves into a representation of one character. (This is a more difficult shared responsibility. They will need an accompanying beat or rhythm to help them to move together.)

Another example of this might be to attempt to recreate the British Airways advertisements where groups of people in separate parts of the room, form the mouth, nose and eyes of a face and then move towards each other to form the whole face. The Music for this was part of The Flower Duet by Delibes from his Opera Lakme.

Group casting

This is where a group of pupils elect to play the same single character collectively but do it in their own way. (This protects each person from undertaking the final isolated responsibility too soon.)

Intermediate Cooperation

At this level again cooperation activities are centred around improving the sense of self as a member of the group and of group cohesion, breaking down barriers of gender, ethnicity etc.

These activities will often throw up problems that are perhaps more covert at other times, and the importance of discussion and debriefing cannot be over emphasised.

The value in doing this work lies in the preparation and analysis of how the class worked as a team. Who was doing most of the work? Who went out of their way to help others? Is there a natural leader in the class or several leaders? How should a leader lead? Was there a sabotage attempt? Did any one grouping dominate another? etc..

Parachute games

<u>Why?</u>
To show that some things can only be achieved by working together.

<u>Organisation:</u>
Whole class outside or in the hall.

<u>Resources:</u>
Parachute. Ball.

<u>How?</u>
1. Begin with everyone standing and holding part of the edge of the parachute.
2. An activity such as swapping places can be done as a warm up.
3. Place the ball on the parachute. Work together to get it to rest in the centre of the parachute. See how many times they can throw the ball in the air and catch it using the parachute.
4. Make a tent out of the parachute by making a dome and then quickly sitting down and tucking the parachute behind them, under their bottoms as they sit down. We have known classes spontaneously burst into song when sitting in their "tent". It is a strange experience for the adult left standing outside the tent!

Cooperative goodies

<u>Why?</u>
To show that cooperation can sometimes mean that everyone benefits.

<u>Organisation:</u>
Only one table with two chairs is to be used for this activity.

<u>Resources:</u>
Small treats, sweets or more healthy alternative.

<u>How?</u>
1. Two pupils sit on the chairs on either side of the table. They put their elbows on the table and grasp each others right hand. The activity looks like arm-wrestling but the teacher should take care that any reference to arm wrestling comes only from the pupils and is not confirmed.
2. The pupils are told that the person whose hand is on top will be given a

"goody", and the main aim of the game is to get the maximum number of goodies to the maximum number of people in the shortest time.

3. Pupils are left to devise their own ways of organising this, with the proviso that only the one table and two chairs can be used at a time and that only one goody is to be given for every hand that is on top.
4. If pupils run it as a contest (which most do) the teacher should emphasise that the group as a whole is losing, with most of them having had no goodies.
5. Eventually someone will suggest that they cooperate which will mean that each pair take it in turns to have their hand on top once and then pass on to the next pair.
6. The activity now shifts from being perceived as a competition to being a group challenge to get everyone as many goodies as possible in the time allocated.

Silent ordering

How?
1. The pupils are asked to get into some sort of order around the circle which may be register order, height or alphabetical order without talking or miming words.
2. Remind them that they need to all be in the right order to be successful. It is not enough to decide your own place in the group.
3. Afterwards, reflect on how well they helped each other and decide how to improve it.

Cooperative pictures

Why?
To encourage small-group cooperation.
To show the value of being given something without asking.

Organisation:
Work in groups on tables.

Resources:
A set of pictures. (see page 85 - 87.)
An envelope and a pair of scissors for each pupil.

How?
1. Seat pupils in groups of 4 - 5 around tables.
2. Give out an envelope and a picture to each pupil.
3. Ask pupils to cut pictures into a number of pieces equal to the number of people in the group.

4. Each pupil then puts a piece of their jigsaw into each envelope. In this way everyone has an envelope with one piece of each of the jigsaws.
5. Each pupil is asked to reconstruct a jigsaw following the rules:
    - do it in silence
    - do not do your own picture
    - give pieces away to help others
    - do not ask for pieces yourself, or signal that you need them
    - do not take pieces from other people.
6. The game is complete when everyone has a completed picture.
7. Discuss the process.

Extensions
Sets of envelopes can be swapped between groups.
Start with one envelope empty.
Start with one envelope containing a completed picture.

Source: Based on an idea from Johnson, D. W. & Johnson, R. T., (1991).

Cooperative knots

Why?
To encourage whole group problem solving.
To encourage positive touching.

Organisation:
Pupils standing in a long line.

How?
1. Pupils begin by holding hands in a long line.
2. The person at the front leads them back on themselves by weaving in and out of the line going in and out of the line going over and under joined hands.
3. They stop when they can go no further and the class have become one knot.
4. The pupils work together to untangle themselves without losing hands.

Cooperative knots 2

Why?
To encourage small group problem solving.

Organisation
Small groups of 6-10 pupils standing in a circle.

How?
1. Pupils close their eyes, put their hands in the middle and grasp the hands of two other people. They must not have the hand of anyone next to them or the two hands of the same person.
2. They then untangle themselves and end in a circle without letting go of the hand they are holding.

This **is** possible! Some people may end up facing backwards.

Number games

Why?
1. To create group spirit and enjoyment.
2. To teach practical mental agility with numbers.

Organisation:
Circle Time.

How?

Fives

1. Everyone begins by standing up. The purpose is to be the last one standing.
2. Count round the circle up to 5 with the first pupil saying 1, the second saying 2 and so on. Pupil number 5 sits down. The next pupil starts again at 1. The main interest of the game is that pupils can choose to say two numbers together e.g. 1+2 or 3+4 in order to keep someone in or get someone out. The last person standing is the winner.
3. Finish with a "go-round" to enable pupils to say what it feels like to have to sit down or knowing that someone got you out on purpose. How could the game be changed so that people don't feel left out.

Spontaneous counting

1. This game is harder the larger the group. Pupils are asked to count to five as a group with individuals calling out one number in the sequence. If two or more pupils call the same number at the same time, the class have to start all over again. No discussion of tactics allowed during the game.
2. This game calls for observational skills, restraint and teamwork.

Fizz Buzz

1. In this activity pupils sit in a circle and count round the circle with each person calling out numbers in sequence. A number, for example five, is

chosen and the group are told that when a multiple of five comes up then the whole class shout "fizz". (1, 2, 3, 4, fizz! 6, 7, 8, 9, fizz!)

2. This activity can be made more difficult by having a fizz number and a "buzz" number. If the two numbers were 5 and 3 for example, 5 would be fizz, 9 would be buzz, and 15 would be fizz-buzz. The aim is to keep counting around the circle for as long as possible.

Sitting on laps

How?
1. The pupils begin by standing in a circle with their shoulders touching.
2. They all turn through 90 degrees so that they are facing each others back.
3. They take hold of the waist of the person in front and slowly sit down.
4. They should all be sitting on each others laps, and they should be quite stable. It is quite hard to do!

Cooperative bodywork

Why?
To create team spirit and enjoyment.
To encourage positive touch.

Organisation:
Pupils in a large space where they can move around freely.

Resources:
P.E. mats.

How?
1. The teacher should refer to the implications for friendship and trust.
2. Pupils sit back to back, feet flat on the floor and knees bent. They attempt to stand up together by pushing against each other.
3. Pupils sit facing each other holding hands with their knees bent, and attempt to stand up by pulling against each other.
4. Pupils do some "donkey leaning". They stand back to back touching at the shoulders and step away from each other slightly, supporting each others' weight.
5. Pupils stand in a circle in groups of six to eight. One pupil is in the middle and with closed eyes and a straight body allows the others in the circle to gently push them around the circle. The others hold their hands at chest height ready to take the pupil's weight and gently push them on.

In order for pupils to have an opportunity to consolidate their learning, they could be asked to devise their own cooperative game and get the class or individuals to play them or they could put on a special event for younger pupils.

Cooperation at Advanced Level

Once basic cooperation skills have been established, the opportunities for using them in a variety of ways are endless.

According to Johnson and Johnson (1989) structuring teaching to ensure cooperation throughout the curriculum leads to a variety of positive learning outcomes:
- Providing each other with efficient and effective help and assistance.
- Exchanging needed resources such as information and materials and processing information more efficiently and effectively.
- Providing each other with feedback in order to improve the subsequent performance of their assigned tasks and responsibilities.
- Challenging each other's conclusions and reasoning in order to promote higher quality decision making and greater insight into problems being considered.
- Advocating the exertion of effort to achieve mutual goals.
- Influencing each other's efforts to achieve the groups goals.
- Acting in trusting and trustworthy ways.
- Being motivated to strive for mutual benefit.
- Having a moderate level of arousal characterised by low anxiety and stress.

Clearly these are outcomes that most teachers would aspire to for both personal, social and academic reasons. Johnson and Johnson are at pains to point out however, that they do not follow automatically from simply requiring young people to work together in groups. They give five basic element, which we have adopted, in order for a lesson to be genuinely cooperative. These are:
- positive interdependence
- individual accountability
- mutual aid
- effective social skills, including decision making, negotiation, leadership etc.
- positive evaluation of each members role within the group, and of the group's success.

Positive interdependence means that group members are linked to each other in a way that ensures that one cannot succeed unless other members of the group succeed (and vice versa) that is, they sink or swim together.

Use the worksheet (page 88) on a lesson by lesson basis to enable group members to be clear about their individual task for the lesson; to facilitate individual accountability and evaluation of each members role within the group; as a summary and written record of group discussion both at the beginning of the session (when differentiated tasks are being negotiated and assigned) and again at the end of the session (when students are supporting each other by reflecting on and evaluating each others contribution in a positive way). These processes will all involve pupils in using and developing their social skills and in helping each other in mutually supportive ways.

Advanced Activities.

Jigsaw learning

Why?
To create a learning environment that requires co-dependency.

Organisation:
Class split into home groups and expert groups.

Resources:
Any resources relating to the curriculum topic used.

How?
1. Introduce topic. Subdivide the topic into areas of study.
2. Form home groups of 4 to 6 pupils. Each pupil in each home group is given one of the topic areas of study in which to become an expert.
3. The experts in each area of study regroup to work together to gather information.
4. The experts return to their home groups to make report and to share in putting their whole set of discoveries together.
5. Each home group presents their work.

Pupil to pupil interviews

Why?
To enable pupils to reflect on and evaluate their work.

Organisation:
Pairwork at the start or end of a lesson.

How?

1. Get pupils into pairs.
2. Ask them to take it in turns to tell their partners:
   - a personal target for the lesson
   - one thing they found easy, difficult or interesting in the previ ous lesson
   - one thing that they did well at the end of a project or lesson
   - one thing they would like to improve on.
3. Partners listen and then repeat back what they heard the other person say.
4. Some pairs might like to feed back to the class.

Extension:

This activity can be extended by asking pupils to formulate targets for a project or term in more detail with their partners help and then to write them down. They can be encouraged to ask each other questions for clarity and reflection. At the end of the project written targets can be reviewed by the same partners.

Conferencing

Why?

To encourage pupil accountability during groupwork.

Organisation :

Small groups.

How?

1. Organise the class to work on a project or topic in small groups.
2. The teacher works with one group for an extended period of time whilst they reflect, not only on the quality and content of the work, but also how they are functioning as a group. They could be encouraged to identify who has been performing a number of roles in the group for example : leader, motivator, information gatherer, time keeper, finisher etc.

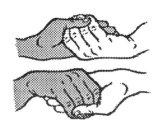

Cooperative pictures

Cooperative pictures

Cooperative pictures

Groupwork sheet

Our group target for _____ (date)

is _____

Name	Task	Evaluation	
		What was done well	What we can do better next time

Chapter 7
Communication and
Emotional Literacy

"As the wail of newborns testifies, babies have intense feelings from the moment they are born. But the newborn's brain is far from fully mature;....only as its nervous system reaches final development - a process that unfolds according to an innate biological clock over the entire course of childhood and into early adolescence - will the child's emotions ripen completely." Daniel Goleman (1996)

We have given a separate section to feelings and emotions partly to prevent this area of the curriculum from becoming subsumed in the development of speaking and listening skills, but mostly to draw attention to the central role which feelings education plays in conflict resolution work and in addition to make the case for it as essential to successful learning outcomes across the whole curriculum and as a crucial life skill.

In both primary and secondary schools we come across many incidents of violence and aggression where pupils strike out in anger because they have misinterpreted neutral messages and expressions as hostile.

Parents and teachers express their concern to us about the lack of impulse control displayed by young people and the prevalence of violent verbal and physical reactions to seemingly minor provocation. In addition, they tell us, there is a tendency for people to act upon hearsay or assumptions and motives which they have heard attributed to individuals.

The activities in this section can be used to reduce violence and to help young people develop:
*   an understanding of themselves and their emotions
*   the ability to express their emotion
*   the ability to read social and emotional cues
*   the ability to make better emotional decisions by controlling the first impulse to act .

The Circle Time work already undertaken will have gone a long way towards encouraging better communication skills and impulse control and will have been invaluable in illuminating the sense of self and of relationships with others. As with other lessons learned in Circle Time, feelings work should be taught in a developmental way, as well as in the course of real events.

Beginner Level

Identifying and labelling feelings

Why?

To develop self awareness and be able to differentiate between feelings.
To have the vocabulary to apply to six basic feelings.
To be able to recognise those feelings in others.

Guess my feeling

How?

1. Teacher introduces six feelings and models the facial expression accompanying the feeling:
    - happy
    - sad
    - angry
    - thoughtful
    - afraid
    - disgusted.
2. Pupils try out the facial expressions for themselves.
3. Teacher hides face and then reveals one of the expressions for pupils to identify.
4. Continue as a guessing game.

Matching games

How?

1. Use the six feelings to make matching games; words with feelings , same faces snap etc.
2. See separate sheet, page 107 - 108.
3. A useful resource to support more work on interpretation of facial expression is the set of feelings cards from Colorcards, Winslow Press, Oxon OX6 0TS.

Pass the face

How?

1. This game is similar to Chinese whispers, but passing a facial expression round the circle hidden behind a book or small board.

Feeling table

How?

    1. Develop a feelings table devoted to one feeling at a time where collections of items, pictures, poems and stories illustrate the feeling.

Cake faces

How?

    1. Instead of baking plain buns or biscuits, pupils decorate them with icing, sugar strands, cherries, currants etc. to depict different facial expressions. Look at them together in the circle and talk about their expressions. (The same could be done with plasticine models.)

Expressing feelings

Why?

    To be able to give expression to feelings and responses.
    To understand other's feeling.

Paintings and drawings of feelings

How?

    1. These can be brought into the circle for the young artist to show and talk about.

Sentence completion go-rounds

How?

    1. Begin sentence completion rounds with:
        • People feel happy (surprised, afraid, angry, etc.) when ...."
        • Something people feel sad about is............."

How are you today?

How?

    1. A circle go-round where each person asks the person on their left,
        • How are you today ...name...? and they reply
        • I feel.......today.

Mumbly muppet

How?

1. A circle go-round to make people laugh, although the object of the game is to try to keep a straight face!
2. Pupils make a "muppet mouth" by covering their teeth with their lips.
3. One pupil turns to the person next to them and says, "I'm Mumbly Muppet, how are you?" and they reply, "Marvellous!" before turning to the next person and repeating, "I'm Mumbly Muppet, how are you?"

Gingerbread feelings

How?

1. A game where the teacher tells the pupils about a number of things which have happened to the gingerbread person and they choose a face to stick onto the blank gingerbread head to express what this has made him/her feel, (see page 109).

Managing feelings

Why?

To realise what is behind a feeling.
To exercise restraint and control impulse.

Why the feeling?

How?

1. Using the Gingerbread figure with a chosen facial expression the Teacher tells pupils "Today , the Gingerbread girl/boy is feeling.................Why do you think s/he's feeling.................?"
2. See "I want it" in the problem solving section and the use of a puppet or mascot in a problem solving go-round in the problem solving section.

Intermediate Level

Identifying and labelling feelings

Why?

To recognise a wider range of feelings and build a vocabulary for them.

| Feelings wall |

How?

1. The pupils brainstorm with a teacher as many feelings as they can think
of. It may help to think of families of words, making lists of words associ-
ated with anger: sadness: fear: enjoyment: love: surprise: disgust: shame:
etc.

2. Here is a prompt list to help the process along:
   - Apologetic, anxious, angry, aggressive, amazed, astonished,
   - Brash, bored, blissful,
   - Critical, curious, confident, cautious, contented, contrite,
   - Delighted, disappointed, depressed, disgusted, dreadful,
   - Energetic, emotional, envious, ecstatic, embarrassed,
   - Friendly, fierce, forceful, frustrated , frightened,
   - Gregarious, grovelling, grieving, guilty,
   - Hopeless, horrified, helpless, hysterical, humiliated,
   - Irritable, indifferent, interested, idiotic,
   - Jealous, joyful, joking,
   - Knowing, kindly,
   - Lonely,
   - Mischievous, miserable, meditative,
   - Negative,
   - Optimistic, obstinate,
   - Perplexed,
   - Relieved, regretful, remorse,
   - Satisfied, shocked, smug, suspicious, sympathetic, scornful,
   - Thoughtful,
   - Undecided,
   - Worried, wonderful,
   - Xenophobic,
   - Young, youthful,
   - Zealous.

3. The teacher should try to ensure that there are positive as well as un-
pleasant feelings.
4. Pupils illustrate all the feelings they have chosen.
5. The feelings are labelled or written up and arranged in a spectrum to form
a display on a wall which is low enough for the pupils to reach.
6. As an ongoing activity throughout the day, pupil volunteers go over to the
wall and point to how they are feeling at the moment.
7. If they want to, they can say why?

How?
1. Pupils can make their own feelings thermometer from a strip of paper about the size of a ruler, by drawing a minimum of five circles to represent faces on its length.
2. They decide individually on a range of feeling going out from the middle face which represents feeling calm and relaxed and then fill in the facial expressions to fit the feelings, writing the word for the feeling under the face.
3. They can indicate how they are feeling on the scale by using a paper clip.
4. The feeling thermometers can be used in Circle Time go-rounds or in pairwork for pupils to identify and express how they are feeling at the time.

Source: Mollie Curry and Carolyn Bromfield (1994).

Feelings graphs

How?
The aim of this activity is to show the pupils that we all feel a full range of feelings throughout the day and that our feelings can change quite quickly. The pupils draw a graph with happy - sad on one axis, and the times of the school day in hours on the other.

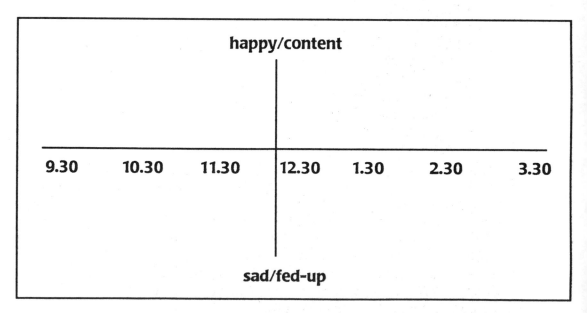

The pupils keep a record throughout the day, and then compare them at the end to find out who was feeling what and when. The graphs can be a useful guide for the teacher to see what parts of the day the pupils most enjoy or dislike.

Based on an idea developed by the Kingston Friends Workshop Group.

Feelings cards

How?
1. In two groups, pupils prepare a set of action cards which all have a sentence beginning "When you............." and a series of feelings cards which all have a sentence beginning "I feel............"on them. An example of an action card might be - When you borrow my pencil without asking, and an example of a feelings card might be - I feel annoyed.
2. The pupils can play a variety of card games with them, one example being that they put all cards face down and take it in turns to try to pick up two that match, for example - When you tell me that you like my hair, with - I feel proud, or - I feel happy. If they pick up two that don't match, for example - When you forget my birthday, with - I feel excited, they have to put both cards back. The winner is the one who has the most pairs after all the cards have been picked up that can be matched.

Expressing feelings

Why?
To be able to name feelings and be able to distinguish between thoughts and feelings.
To respect differences in how people feel about things.

Organisation:
Circle Time

One to ten

How?
1. In Circle Time as a go-round pupils give a score to how they are feeling at the moment from 1 to 10 and explain why in a sentence. This is a very powerful exercise in helping to develop empathy. If the teacher feels that individual pupils with low scores are in need of peer support then one of the problem solving techniques from the next section may be useful.
2. After commenting that some of us are feeling very low today pupils could be asked to say what help they could offer each other in a straightforward go-round. This exercise is also a good evaluation tool to use at the start of an affirmation session. Repeat it again at the end and notice how many scores have gone up as a result of feeling valued and appreciated.

I feel...

How?

1. Teacher mentions something topical or an issue or a common experience for the pupils and asks, " How do you feel about that? " or "How did you feel about that?" (not "What do you think of that?") Pupils respond in a go-round without commenting on each others responses. They may need support if offering judgments or opinions instead of feelings, e.g. " I feel it should be stopped." ... instead of " I feel irritated by that."

Experiences might include:

My first day at school. The first time I went to the swimming baths. When I go to the dentists or doctors. The day before Eid or Diwali or Christmas or Hanukah. The day after my birthday. A new baby in our family. When I get told off. When I am left out or left behind.

Imaginary experiences might include:

"How would you feel if...... you were asked to walk across a high wire, to go up into space, to go down under the earth, to open a mystery parcel, to tell someone their party was cancelled, you woke up and your hair had turned blue."

Topics:

- The affect the weather has on us.
- Other people in the world not having enough to eat.
- Street children in Brazil.
- Intensive farming.
- Hens kept in battery cages.
- Bears made to dance for people's entertainment.
- Life in outer space.
- The National Lottery.

2. Finish with a summary of the range of feelings. Draw attention to people's right to their own feelings.
3. An adaptation of this would be to play a variety of music invoking different moods, read short poems, or smell aroma therapy oils to see if they affect our feelings.

Intonation

How?

1. In a go-round pupils pass on phrases such as "What are you doing?" "Where are you going?" or even just "Hello" with each person trying to use different intonation to give the words or phrase a different meaning.

Body language

How?
1. In pairs pupils decide how you can tell if someone is angry (or happy, sad, indifferent etc.) and they feedback in a go-round starting "We think........"
2. Discussion about body language and non-verbal communication.
3. In pairs pupils attempt to find a way of communicating one message verbally at the same time as giving another different message non-verbally.
4. Share some of these and guess what the messages are.
5. Pupils could go on to identify how to tell the difference between an intentionally hostile encounter and an accidental one.
6. Use role playing to explore the differences.

Managing feelings

Why?
To understand what is behind a feeling.
To develop strategies to change or redirect an emotional response.
To control impulse.

Organisation:
Small groupwork and Circle Time.

Resources:
Pencil and paper for note taking.

How feelings affect us

How?
1. Focus on one feeling at a time, selected perhaps from the way some members of the class are feeling at the moment.
2. In small groups pupils discuss and make notes:
   - What makes us feel that way?
   - What happens to us and our bodies when we feel that way?
   - How can you tell if another person is feeling the same way?
   - What can we do about this feeling if we want to change it?
3. Groups report back to the main circle.
4. Booklets can be produced from these recommendations.
"What you can do if you're feeling..................."

The problem solving techniques in the next chapter will help to give a framework for working through frustrations and difficulties, controlling impulsive reaction.

Knowing the difference between feelings and actions

Why?
To begin to understand the links between feeling, thought and reaction.

| Feeling, thought, reaction |

How?
1. As a whole group pupils brainstorm common things which people in school say and do to or for each other. Divide the list into helpful and unhelpful things, e.g.

helpful	**unhelpful**
lends me a rubber	won't share the felt pens
says, 'I like your drawing'	says, 'That looks stupid', to your drawing
tells me a joke	tells tales about me

2. Choosing two helpful and two unhelpful things, pupils discuss in pairs :
   - how these things make them feel
   - what they are then likely to think about the person saying or doing whatever it is
   - what their usual response is.
3. They jot down responses on a check list.

If someone...	we feel...	we think...	then we...

4. In the same pairs, take turns to role play the four actions or sayings. Practice just saying how you feel without reacting to your thoughts.
5. Circle go-round:
   - What was easy or hard about that?
   - What were some of the feelings people had to say?
   - What would happen if everyone reacted to all their thoughts and feelings?
6. Brainstorm what society would be like. Imagine how it would affect shopping, television programmes, teachers and pupils in schools, judges in courts, footballers, dancers and musicians, airline pilots and bus drivers.

7. Choose an example to role play in small groups. Do it in two ways. First where everyone reacts to their feelings and thoughts, secondly where they just express how they are feeling.
8. Share some of these and have a final go-round to comment on what people have learned and what they did well.
9. Continue with the exercises in the problem solving chapter designed to address the problem and avoid attacking the person.

Advanced Level

Peer relationships take on immense importance in pupils' lives. They have more ambiguous social realities and need the ability to take multiple perspectives and to make relationships work better.

Identifying and labelling feelings

Why?
To develop a deeper awareness of the range of feelings and moods.
To be able to read and respond to social and emotional cues from others.

| Detector tune- in |

How?
1. Pupils sitting in a circle. Half a dozen volunteer pupils leave the circle and turn their backs on the others, they are the outsiders.
2. Those left in the circle silently appoint a leader and begin by all tapping their knees continuously until the leader takes over and signals a change of action e.g. clapping hands, pointing with thumbs over shoulders, raising arms up and down. They must follow the leader as closely as possible but try to make it difficult for anyone to guess who the leader is.
3. The outsiders now rejoin the circle and as quickly as possible join in the actions.
4. Can they guess who the leader is? If it was easy, how could it be made more difficult? What are the give away signals?
5. Swap "outsiders" if they wish. Try it again and this time make the movements and signals smaller and more subtle.
6. Try it again but this time as well as picking a leader decide on one category of group members e.g. all those with lace-up shoes, all those with blue eyes or grey jumpers and one action which they do not copy e.g. folding their arms or patting their heads.
7. When the outsiders enter the circle they join in as usual but this time they

have to identify not only the leader but also the "tribe" within the group who do not copy one of the leaders actions. If they identify themselves as belonging to that tribe they stop when the tribe do.

8. Discuss what skills they were using and what they did well. What are the kind of signals we can pick up if we want to join a group, say at dinner time or socially?

9. They could role play a hostile group and a welcoming group, or outsiders who can tune in quickly to the group and ones who can't, and share the results.

Stake out

Resources:
A set of activity and mood cards (pages 110 - 111).

How?
1. There are teams of four who are about to be joined by two outsiders.
2. The circumstances and activity of the group of four are selected from cards and so is their mood. Then select one activity card and one mood card for each group of four.
3. They begin an interaction according to the cards they have selected e.g. mending a broken window, miserably, or delicate brain surgery quietly but cheerfully, or assembling a house of cards, with gusto, effusively.
4. The outsiders observe them for 1 minute and then must decide upon emotions and style of interacting before attempting to join the team in their activity.
5. Groups discuss how successfully the outsiders fitted themselves into the team and how accurately they responded to the mood and activity of the team.
6. Swap roles and have another go.
7. Finish with a go-round of general observations about the most successful strategies for becoming accepted into the team and the ones which caused the team to reject the outsiders.
8. Does this sound familiar or true to them?
   • When people are joining teams or established groups of people they very often hang back and observe how the group interacts and what the group values or is going to do next.
   • Then they align their mood, speech and style to the group's and wait for an opportunity to quietly help the group with its next move.
   • Groups often reject people who misinterpret the group's intentions or try to change what the group are doing or the way they are doing it. In other words people who don't tune in

and fit in but who try to take over or do things differently, are rejected.

• Once people are accepted as one of the group they can make suggestions about different ways of doing things or assert their own skills......but not until then.

Feeling - predicaments

Resources
A set of response cards and predicament cards (pages 112 - 113).

How?
1. In pairs. One listener and one speaker. Two sets of cards for the class. One set has responses (emotions and moods), one set has predicaments.
2. The speaker in each pair takes one card from each pile. This will give them a predicament and an emotional response. e.g. Predicament: You are homeless because your house has just burned down. Emotion: You are overjoyed. They must think of a reason for their emotion to make sense of it in the light of their predicament.
3. They speak to the listener who uses S.A.R.A.H.
    • Stop talking.
    • Active listening.
    • Repeat back what you are told.
    • Accept how the person is feeling.
    • Help them to decide what they want to do about things
    (see Advanced Speaking and Listening skills.)
   to discover what their predicament is and to help them express their feelings.
4. Feedback from speaker in the pair to listener in the pair. "The things you did well were.........What would make it even better would be ....".
5. Feedback in the circle from pairs. " What we did well was...... What we found difficult was.......What we would do differently next time........"
6. Discuss in the circle the kinds of questions that were the most useful in helping to clarify and explore the problem and feelings of the speaker. (See Advanced Mediation section for information about open and closed questions.)
7. Swop roles and repeat with a new set of cards for the speaker.
8. Evaluate and feedback in the same way.

Expressing feelings

<u>Why?</u>
To be able to monitor what those around us are feeling.

<u>Organisation:</u>
Pairwork.

Reading faces

<u>How?</u>
1. Discuss what we might look for if we were reading someone's face to understand their feelings or thoughts. e.g.
   brows;   furrowed , smooth, frowning.
   eyes;   rolling down or up, looking left or right.
   nostrils;   flaring, twitching.
   lips;   curling, pressed together.
   skin;   tightening, slackening.
   breathing; slowing, accelerating, deepening.
2. In pairs each person is asked to identify three specific incidents in which they felt:
   - exhilarated
   - happy
   - saddened (this should not be a deeply upsetting experience or trauma).
3. Partners sit facing each other. One is asked to close their eyes and recall the three incidents (in any order they choose) and their accompanying feelings one after the other. The other becomes an observer watching their partners facial movements.
4. Observers identify the order in which their partner chose to recall the incidents. They may swap over or try them again in a different order.
5. Discussion: What observations did you make? What did you find difficult? What did you gain from the exercise? Subtle messages are constantly given by others which we may not be aware of, although we may be subconsciously affected.

Source: Nic Fine and Fiona Macbeth (1990).

Managing feelings and controlling impulse

<u>Why?</u>
To learn ways to manage anger, anxiety and stress.

Three to one

How?

1. Pupils write down an incident or situation they faced recently at school or socially.
2. Divide into small groups and choose one persons situation to work on.
3. Role play the situation in three ways:
    - the most likely response
    - the most provocative response
    - the "successful" response which works at the time (not neces sarily universal).
4. Share some of these as a whole group or between groups.
5. Discuss: differences made by approaches; how did they determine whether an approach was successful? skills or tactics used to avoid provocative response; skills and tactics used in the most "successful" response.

Source: Nic Fine and Fiona Macbeth (1990).

Anger bubbles

How?

1. In a Circle Time go-round, respond to the question "what makes you angry?" followed by "what do you do when you're angry?"
2. Put the headings on the blackboard / flipchart.
    - Why am I angry?
    - Who am I angry with?
    - How angry am I on a scale of 1 to 10?
    - What am I going to do?
3. Suggest that learning to answer these questions before acting is a useful skill.
4. In triads ask them to decide on an example of something which makes each of them angry and to take turns to role play the examples using the four "anger bubbles" before responding. In other words their partners recreate for them the usual situation which provokes them to anger and they must answer (silently or out loud whichever they prefer) the four questions in the bubbles before responding.
5. Discussion : How might answering these questions help you to express your anger effectively? Why might ranking your anger from 1 to 10 help? What are some ways of expressing anger safely for everyone? What can you do if you are angry with any particular person? What have people found to be helpful ways of calming down?

Source: William J. Kreidler (1984).

Resource:
   Underlying feelings activity sheet (page 114).

How?
   1. Angry. - Pupils write down in one sentence a situation at school when they felt really angry.
   2. Hurt. - Explain that a layer of hurt often underlies anger. Ask everyone to write a sentence about the hurt behind their anger. "I felt hurt because nobody asked before they took my graphics equipment."
   3. Needs - The reason for hurt is often unmet need. Ask everyone to write a sentence about their needs in the same instance. "I need to be considered and valued."
   4. Fears - Along side the need are often fears. Ask pupils what fears may lie behind the anger, and write a sentence about them. "I worry that people will just ride rough shod over me or treat me as if I didn't exist."
   5. In pairs share the sentences.
   6. Discussion. What's the value of understanding what lies behind anger? In what way does knowing this help us to deal with or face the anger of others?

Source: Nic Fine and Fiona Macbeth (1990).

The problem solving techniques in the next chapter will help to provide a safe framework for managing impulsive responses.

Knowing the difference between feelings and actions

Why?
   To know if thoughts or feelings are ruling a decision.
   To be able to distinguish what someone says and does and your own reaction.

Red flags

Resource:
   Red flag activity sheet (page 115).

How?
   1. Give each person a copy of the red flags sheet and ask them to fill it in.
   2. In pairs share what they want to from their lists. Then choose one emo-

tion each to enact together.

3. Pairs show their examples (whole group or small groups). Others guess to which red flag each scene relates.

4. Discussion: What does this exercise teach you about yourself? How could anticipating your usual reaction help? What is helpful about seeing other people's red flags?

Source: Nic Fine and Fiona Macbeth (1990).

Ideal enemies

How?

1. The class is split into groups of six. Each group is given a large cardboard label with a ribbon tied to it and asked to create an "ideal enemy" by writing the characteristics of their "enemies" onto the label.

2. They should focus on behaviour by writing down the sorts of things that people around them do that get them annoyed, such as pushing into the dinner queue, or calling people names.

3. They then ask a volunteer from the group to have the label around their neck and to mime some of the actions from the list for the other groups to see, whilst someone else in the group reads from the label. You can use dressing up clothes and props to add authenticity!

4. When the hilarity has died down the pupils are asked to get back into their groups and to cross off the list on the label anything that anyone in the group still does or has done in the past. The result is usually that almost everything on the list is crossed off so that the pupils are left with the idea that we often project onto others the things that we least like about ourselves.

5. The facilitator could point out that the only way to really know what someone is like is to talk to them and find out about them rather than looking at what they do and making judgments about them.

Based on an idea developed by the LEAP Confronting Conflict.

Hidden thoughts

How?

1. Decide as a group on some common conversations or exchanges they have with other people such as teachers, parents, siblings or each other.

2. In groups of four divide into Voice 1 and Thoughts 1. Voice 2 and Thoughts 2.

3. Voice 1 cannot speak until Thought 1 has spoken. Voice 2 cannot speak until Thought 2 has spoken.

4. Choose a conversation between Voices 1 and 2. They will have to carry on this conversation listening to their own thoughts first, considering what the other voice says and summing up the situation before speaking.
5. Choose a fairly "light" topic of conversation for the first trial in order to get the communication flow between the four group members going well

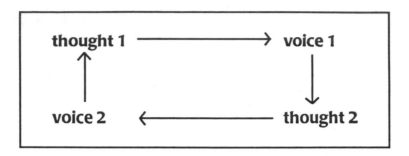

6. After this initial practice spend 4 minutes on each of 4 role plays, swapping roles if wanted.
7. Discussion: Why do we not express our thoughts openly? What are the blocks about expressing our feelings? How can we tell when someone is concealing a thought or feeling?

Source: Nic Fine and Fiona Macbeth (1990).

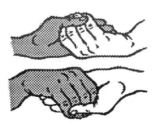

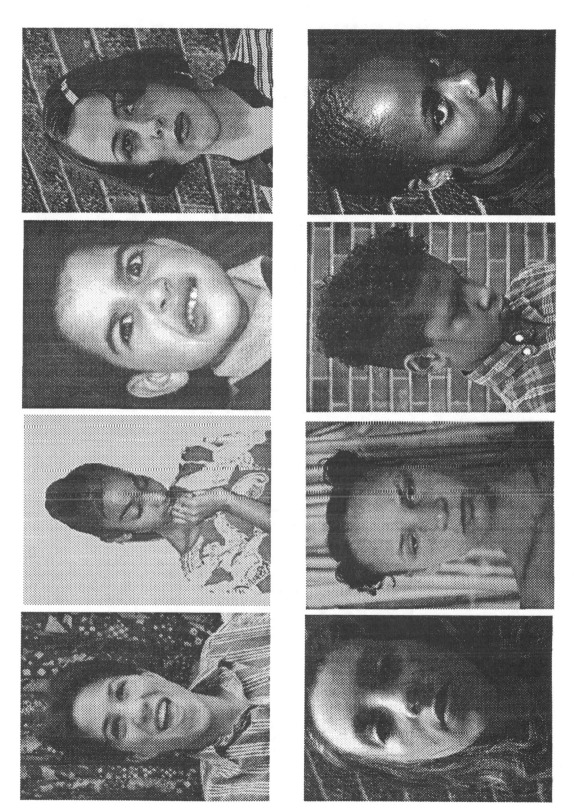

Thoughtful

Happy

Disgusted

Sad

Afraid

Angry

Activity cards

mending a broken window

delicate brain surgery

assembling a house of cards

bathing a Chihuahua (tiny dog)

gathering wood and making a camp fire

practising a synchronised swimming routine

laying the table for a banquet of 100 people

catching mice

laying a huge stair carpet

watering tomato plants

Mood cards

miserably	quietly
cheerfully	with gusto
effusively	fearfully
furtively	depressed
mournfully	tranquil
relaxed	jubilant
concentration	gracefully
poetically	irritable

Predicament cards

You are homeless because your house has just burned down.

You have just heard that you have won the National Lottery.

Your friend has won an art competition using your drawing.

Your pet alligator is too big to keep in a tank in your house.

Your mother says you must wear your brothers old clothes.

You have found the key to the school safe in your bag.

An experiment you did shows you how to reverse aging.

You have just heard that your mother has been chosen to play the lead in the school musical instead of you.

An elderly relative invites you on holiday to Disney World with the over 60's club.

You agreed to look after your friends pets while they were away over the weekend and they have all escaped.

Response cards

You feel devastated.

You are overjoyed.

You are thrilled to bits.

You feel appalled.

You are confused and unhappy.

You are positively delighted.

You are shocked.

You are completely horrified.

You are really anxious and worried.

You are pleasantly surprised.

Underlying Anger

I felt really angry when..

I felt hurt because...

I need...

I am worried that...

Red Flag sheet

What people/things/situations make me angry?

What people/things/situations frighten or upset me?

What sort of behaviour/gestures/words make me switch off?

What situations/things/people irritate me?

What makes me uneasy?

What people/situations/things make me frustrated.

Source: Nic Fine and Fiona Macbeth (1990).

115

CHAPTER 8
Problem Solving and
Conflict Resolution

The importance of the curriculum work in affirmation, communication (particularly expressing feelings and asserting needs) and cooperation will be apparent throughout this chapter. To approach competence in conflict resolution skills, young people need a developed sense of themselves as a member of a group or team, vocabulary, recognition and understanding of feelings, the ability to express needs, empathy and a willingness to consider another point of view. If you are tempted to go straight to the chapter on mediation without due preparation, we would urge you to delay making a start on this section until a basis of trust, and mutual respect is established and until speaking, listening and feelings awareness are sufficiently developed.

Pupils of all ages can be helped to understand that conflict is not in itself wrong/bad/horrible. It is not wrong to want different things: to want to play football or basketball and run noisily about rather than walking or sitting quietly, to want to go on riding the tricycle and not swap for the scooter, to have different opinions or beliefs or tastes in music, dress or pastimes. It is the way that we respond to these conflicts of interest that matters. Johnson and Johnson (1991) say that negotiation begins the moment when you communicate to the other person that there is a conflict and you want to resolve it. We are about to discover that conflict can be a creative force for good.

At each stage whether Primary or Secondary, the journey towards dispute resolution and mediation skills needs to cover:
*   an understanding of conflict
*   an awareness of personal conflict styles
*   an appreciation of the effects of conflict
*   the ability and willingness to see another point of view
*   practise at generating win/win solutions
*   shared development of strategies - personal, group and whole school
*   a way of consistently reviewing and renegotiating decisions.

We can follow the steps of the mediation process itself in order to cover these elements of dispute resolution:
Step 1 Keep the ground rules for working together.
Step 2 Identify and understand what is happening.
Step 3 Hear and acknowledge the impact. Look at it from the other person's point of view.

Step 4 Pool suggestions of what can be done.
Step 5 Agree a mutually acceptable way forward.

What follows is a series of activities that can be used to develop pupil's skills for each step. Once the skills have been learnt and rehearsed in hypothetical situations pupils can begin to use them in real life situations.

Step 1 - Ground rules. Rights and responsibilities

<u>Why?</u>
   To reinforce agreed codes of conduct towards each other.
   To place conflict resolution work in a context.
   To begin to consider positive outlets for needs manifesting themselves in
      antisocial ways.

<u>Organisation:</u>
   Circle Time format with groupwork.

<u>How?</u>
   1. Use a Circle Time go-round for pupils to refresh each others memories
      about the rights and responsibilities agreed as their class or school code.
      (see chapter 2, How to use this book.)
    2. Tell them that all of the problem solving and conflict resolution work we
      are going to do, will be helping to uphold those rights and responsibilities.
      e.g. the right to feel safe, the right to be spoken to with respect, the re-
      sponsibility to avoid using violence, the responsibility to treat others with
      respect. The aim is to find a way of helping everyone to meet their needs
      without infringing the rights of others. This will include finding outlets for
      physical energy and the need for machismo and self importance through
      positive means.
   3. Mixing game.
   4. Pairwork; discuss why people boss other people around and what they
      want to get out of it.
   5. Go-round reporting back with the sentence starting " We both think ...."
   6. Teacher or pupil summarises the go-round and lists main reasons for
      behaviour.
   7 Mixing game.
   8. Small groupwork. Suggestions of ways for people who boss others to
      meet their needs without oppressing others and to use their leadership
      skills for the good of the group or school.
   9. Circle report back and discussion of what other support we could offer to
      help someone to become more cooperative.
   10. Summary and closing game.

Step 2a - Understanding conflict. What is it that happens?

Why?

To gather a picture of conflicts which occur in school without personalising them.

To help pupils to disclose information safely.

To ascertain the exact nature of bullying behaviour in the class or school.

Organisation:

A combination of Circle Time and groupwork.

Use mixing games

How?

1. Silent Statements. (Bliss, T. and Tetley, J. 1993)
   - "Stand up and change places if...."

Distance disclosures to begin with, so that they remain general and unthreatening but refer to specific bullying behaviours and not to bullying as a global term.
   - "...you know arguments have turned into fights at some time in this school."
   - "....sometime in this class"
   - "...you know someone who has fallen out this week/last week..."
   - "...you know someone who has had an argument this week which ended badly,.."
   - "...you know someone got into a fight this week..."

2. Invite other "ifs" on the topic of conflict....
3. Finish with a go-round for people to comment on what they noticed or realised but not to comment on individual responses.

The spectrum activity

How?

1. The rules are:
   - The wall at one end of the room means "a lot" or "it has happened a lot".
   - A spot half way between the two walls means "a bit "or "it sometimes happens".
   - The opposite wall means "never" or "it never happens"
2. The teacher calling responses stands along the length of the room and not at either end.

<u>Note</u>

We have seen this activity tried in the circle with the centre of the circle meaning "a lot", a radius out from the centre meaning "sometimes" and a seat round the edge meaning "never".

This is <u>not</u> a good way of using this activity. Responses become biased because the circle arrangement focuses attention on one answer more than others. So, for example, a child who always has hurtful words said to them, or who experiences most conflict would be required to move to the centre of the circle into the focus of the group.

However, in a linear spectrum with everyone facing forwards towards the teacher or caller, exposure is minimised and pupils may feel safer to respond genuinely.

3. Pupils move to one of the spots according to their response to a series of statements which start

"In this school this term ...."

"In this class over the last two weeks..........."

4. Then give examples of particular behaviours that you are wishing to focus on

   • "If someone bigger than you pushed in front of you or took advantage of their size."

   • "If someone treated something that you did accidentally as if it had been done on purpose."

5. Give pupils the chance to call out statements to gain information about how common various experiences are.

6. Finish with a go round for people to comment on what they noticed or realised but not to comment on individual responses.

<u>Extension:</u>

This activity can be used to facilitate discussion or debate about particular issues by beginning with a statement such as,

   • "If someone hits you, you should hit them back."

   • "We should bring back capital punishment for violent crimes."

Pupils take their position along the spectrum and are then asked to find someone who is at least five places away from them on the spectrum in either direction and then to put their own case and find out why the other person thinks as they do.

The spectrum activity can be repeated at the end to find out if anyone has moved their position.

Finally there can be discussion about how they handled the debate with their partner, what they found difficult and what they did well.

How arguments and fights make us feel

Resources:
   Give out sticky labels or small pieces of paper and pencils or pens.

Organisation:
   Pupils do not need to be in a circle for this activity, but the quality of the
      silent reflection and sense of shared experience is enhanced by sitting in a
      circle.

How?
   1. Create silence and stillness.
   2. Ask pupils to reflect on a conflict situation (an argument or fight perhaps)
      which has involved them personally and to try to remember and put a
      name to the feelings they experienced while it was happening.
   3. Each person then writes or draws their feelings on a small piece of paper
      or sticky label
   4. Still maintaining the silence, the label, drawing or explanation is then put
      anonymously into a container or attached to a paper figure.
   5. Into the silence someone reads back to the group or interprets from the
      drawings all the feelings expressed.
   6. Another way of doing this is for people's original contributions to be
      mixed up and redistributed round the circle. Then, in a go-round, people
      read the paper or label they have been given.
   7. Discuss what we have learnt.
   8. Make the point that strong feelings are aroused in conflicts and feelings
      are as important as facts. Feelings ARE facts.
   9. If this is the end of the session, it will be important to finish on a positive
      note or with an activity that is fun. Which game would they like to play?

Extension:
   Use all the "P's ".. Pictures, poses, puppets, prose, poetry to enable pupils to
      express the range of conflicts that are occurring in school.
   Drama presentations can include soft toys or puppets for younger pupils and
      tableaux for older ones.

Tableaux

Why?
   To provide a controlled, clear way of seeing and hearing what is happening
      without exposing individuals and without play fighting or argument taking
      over.

<u>Organisation:</u>
Work in small groups of 3 or 4.

<u>How?</u>
Preparation:
1. Groups choose a familiar or common conflict situation.
2. One person uses the other group members as moveable statues to represent the action.
3. That person also narrates what is being said and done by the statues in the situation.

Presentation:
1. The ground rules of Circle Time apply (only those presenting may speak. No put-downs) and observers are asked to try to pick out what the conflict of interest is and to notice what the group presenting are doing well.
2. Silent count downs (3.2.1. with fingers) and signals for stop and go ('As if in a Radio Station') will help to create and maintain the right focused atmosphere between presentations.
3. Facilitator and pupils list the common occurrences seen and say what they are about i.e. friendship, possessions, territory. (It will be useful to keep a list of these examples of conflict to use in later exercises.)
4. Pairwork using reflective listening (see advanced speaking and listening section) to share 'A time in school when I was involved in an argument'
5. A circle go-round to make any comments on the different kinds of conflict. Are any of them any better than others?

Source Leaveners Arts Project Mediation UK Conference.

Step 2b - Understanding conflict - Developmental Stages

"Children and young people go through definable stages in the development of their ability to negotiate." (Presland, J. 1996.)

Defining the problem
- **Level 0** He won't give me the ball.
- **Level 1** We both want the ball, but I'm out to get it.
- **Level 2** We both want the ball but I need to persuade him to give it to me. Perhaps I can do something in exchange.
- **Level 3** We both want the ball. Perhaps we can work out together how both of us can have some of what we want.

When it comes to ways of solving conflicts at first strategies are mainly physical and impulsive. Then they become more psychological;

- balancing assertion and submission
- attempting to satisfy conflicting needs
- collaborating to achieve shared goals.

- **Level 0** - I'll grab.
- **Level 1** - I'll make him give it to me. I might have to threaten or hit him.
- **Level 2** - I'll suggest I have it for a while, then he can have it. Maybe I'll swap him something for it.
- **Level 3** - We can play together or decide who needs it most at the moment.

Yeates and Selman (1989) propose the steps be taught and practised using hypothetical conflict situations at first in pairs or groups. The pupils' level in the developmental scheme above should be assessed. Teaching should then be focused on the next step up. Pupils are encouraged to consider the consequences of each strategy and to evaluate the outcome.

What I want, why I want it

Why?
  To rehearse the language of early negotiation skills.
  To begin to develop win/win solutions.

Organisation:
  Pupils in Circle.

Resources:
  A desirable object or mascot.
  The following formula:
  - Say "I want........"
  - Say why.
  - Say how you're feeling.
  - Make a suggestion.
  - Agree what to do so that it is fair, (win/win).

It will be helpful to have a note of this on the blackboard or on a big piece of paper in the middle of the circle as a reminder until people are familiar with it.

How?
  1. Teacher introduces an object to the group (e.g. set of headphones, computer disc, basketball, bubble bath liquid, book, bag etc.) and asks them to

imagine that this is something that they all badly want to use. It belongs to the class.

2. One person is given the object to hold. They are partnered with someone sitting directly opposite them across the circle. They take it in turn to say the formula, starting with the person holding the object who says,

"I want it ......"

The person sitting opposite across the circle also then says, "I want it"

The person holding the object says why they want it.

The person sitting opposite says why they want it.

The person holding the object expresses feelings about the other person wanting the object.

The person opposite expresses feelings.

The person with the object suggests how to solve things fairly.

The person opposite responds with a suggestion.

They try to reach a win/win solution.

It may go something like this.....

Paul (with tape) "I want it."

Pete (without tape) "I want it."

Paul   "I want to listen to it to cheer me up."

Pete   "I haven't heard it yet, so I want to listen to it now."

Paul   "I feel fed up."

Pete   "I feel frustrated."

Paul   "I could listen to it for half an hour and then give it to you."

Pete   "Well, I need to listen to it now because Eastenders is on in half an hour. I would miss it. I could have it to listen to for half an hour then give it to you."

Paul   "Or we could listen to it together now."

Pete   "O.K."

Paul   "O.K."

3. The object is passed round the circle and each time the person opposite and the person holding it state their needs and their feelings and try to reach agreement until everyone has had a go.
4. Remind pairs of the need to try to find a solution that is fair to both.
5. Encourage pupils to discuss interactions and solutions
6. Ask why it is important to try to negotiate a fair solution. What would happen if we were all trying to win all of the time?

It is important to know people's feelings and the reasons so that these can be taken into account during negotiation. This isn't just something to use when we want an object someone else has. It can help people who want all sorts of things, like a teacher or parent who wants someone to tidy up or a person who wants to work quietly without interruptions.

Step 2c - How do we usually respond? Conflict styles

Fist and palm exercise and conflict questionnaire

Why?

    To reflect on our own preferred response to conflict.
    To become aware of the range of responses available to us.
    To consider appropriate ways of responding to different situations.

Organisation:

    Pupils seated in a circle.

Resources:

    A copy of the questionnaire for each pupil. Pencils.

How?

1. Begin with a mixing game such as "I love my friends"
2. In pairs. One person curls hand into a fist.
3. The other partner in the pair has exactly one minute to get their partner to uncurl their hand and show a palm.
4. After one minute stop the pairs. Swap roles and repeat the exercise.
5. At the end of a further minute stop the pairs.
6. In a go-round comment on what strategies your partner used to get you to show a palm, and say whether it was successful.
7. Summarise the range of strategies used. These are likely to include, forcing, distracting, coercing or bribing, using humour, "fibbing" etc.
8. Make the point that all of these strategies have their uses. Whether they are successful will depend on how appropriate they are to the situation and the people involved.
9. In 3's try to come up with some examples of situations where it would be important to use one of the approaches tried out in the pairwork.
10. Feedback in a go-round and then summarise. "So what we are saying is that....." (hopefully they will make the points themselves about the difference between acting when personal safety or the rights of someone younger or weaker are involved and acting to try to reach a compromise.)
11. Before going on to do the questionnaire it would be helpful to pupils if they agree on one particular example of a conflict to have in mind as they answer the questions.
12. Give out the conflict questionnaire sheet and go over the explanation of how to answer it and add up the scores, activity pages 135 - 137.
13. Pupils answer the questionnaire individually.
14. In pairs share the results discussing whether you agree with the outcome and saying what you understand to be your usual way of dealing with conflict.

15. In a go-round pupils comment as they wish on their findings.
16. Further go-rounds can respond to questions such as:
- "What difference would it have made to the way you answered the questionnaire if the chosen conflict situation had been about something else?"
- "Would our way of responding be different if we were in conflict with people much older or younger than us? ...adults or toddlers perhaps?"
- "When would it be inappropriate or dangerous to use certain responses?"
- "What happens when people get stuck with one way of reacting?"

In the final summing up make the point that what matters is that we should be able to choose from a range of different responses...like having a tool box to select the right tool for the job from.

Pupils may want to identify which of the "styles" or ways of responding they would like to do more work on or have more support with. This can be done as pairwork again if desirable, reporting back "We would both like help with......"

Source: Thomas and Kilman, (1990) and Johnson and Johnson (1991).

Step 2d - Understanding conflict

| The ingredients of conflict |

Why?
  To consider what usually happens when two people argue or fight.
  To raise awareness of ways of changing the focus of a verbal attack.
  To arrive at a set of ground rules for resolving conflict.

Organisation:
  Pupils gathered where they can see items on the floor and whole group
    recordings on paper or blackboard.

Resources:
  Two items to represent two disputants, ball and skittle.
  One item to represent their problem, beanbag.
  A way of drawing or placing 2 arrows between items.
  Small pieces of paper to write on.

How?

1. Arrange the items to represent the model below

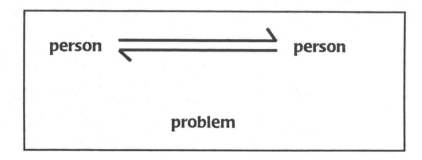

2. Explain that what usually happens is that people put all of their energies during an argument into attacking the other person and very little energy into sorting out the actual cause of the problem represented by the bean-bag (or whatever is representing the problem). Point the arrows between the two people to represent the focus of their attack.
3. Ask pupils to indicate what happens between the two people in a fight or argument by writing words on slips of paper, or by calling out for the teacher to write the words. The range of responses usually includes all or most of the following

> ♦ shouting ♦ swearing
> ♦ insults ♦ blaming
> ♦ hitting ♦ threatening
> ♦ interrupting each other
> ♦ trying to have the last word
> ♦ trying to hurt their feelings
> ♦ trying make them give in.

4. Discuss why all of these things are used, what is each person trying to do in this argument. Why? Make the point that in this way of doing things people expect there will be a winner and a loser.
5. Ask what would we need to take away to change the focus from attacking the person to attacking the problem? Move the arrows so that they point at the item representing the problem.

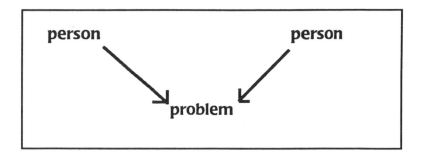

6. Take away the pieces of paper as pupils mention them. And what do we need to put in place of each of these? Replace them as pupils mention them.

| shouting | will replaced by | listening |
| interrupting | will replaced by | taking turns to speak |

and so on.

7. What pupils will have arrived at by the end of this process are the prerequisites for all conflict resolution and problem solving techniques and in particular the ground rules used in the mediation process:
   - no blaming
   - talk about yourself
   - no interrupting
   - take turns to speak
   - no swearing or name calling
   - use the other person's proper name.
8. Do these ground rules look familiar to anyone? They have been practising them regularly in Circle Time.

Attacking the problem, not the person

Why?
  To rehearse alternative language.

Organisation:
  Circle Time with pair and small groupwork.

Resources:
  Prompt sheets page 138.

How?
  1. Recap on the previous exercise "Ingredients of conflict".

2. Either use examples of conflict situations previously identified by pupils in their earlier work or brainstorm a number of choices.
3. Explain that the focus of the session is to find the words to attack the problem instead of the person. First to make a note of some of these then to try them out.
4. Go over the prompt sheet so that everyone understands how to fill it in.
5. In pairs decide on two conflicts and fill in the words to identify the behaviour or actions causing the problem. Say, politely and clearly, what you have seen and heard without judgment:
    • how you are feeling about it
    • why you are feeling this way and what you need
    • what action you would like.
6. In a go-round share some of the finished examples.
7. Next in 3's have an observer and two people who have fallen out. Try out ways of saying things to each other without blaming or attacking each other. The observer could give an agreed signal to indicate when they have managed this and when they have slipped into blame.
8. Give pupils the chance to swap places and all have a go at observing etc.
  Give them the time and space to make mistakes and try things out. This is a very challenging exercise. Several opportunities may be needed before they feel that they are getting the hang of things.
9. A final go-round could just invite people to comment on how they got on.
10. Finish with an affirmation activity to remind pupils what skills they already have.

Extension:
   Assertiveness exercises that encourage pupils to speak for themselves and say "I" instead of "you"
   Swapping chairs in the rehearsal of new language to take the other persons part.

Step 3 - Seeing things differently

Why?
   To develop empathy and the ability to see different perspectives on an issue.
   To appreciate the difficulties caused by assumptions.

Resources:
   Any illustration, photograph or advertisement, role play slips, red and blue summary sheets, pencils.

Picture it

How?
1. Show the pupils the selected picture.
2. Ask pupils to decide on two things which they think are important or interesting about the picture.
3. Have a go-round to discuss what people feel is most important or interesting about the picture?
4. Make the point that people see things in very different ways and experience things in different ways. It is important to know what we see and hear and feel and to be aware of our reasons for wanting or doing things... but it is also important to try to understand how other people see, hear and feel things and to try to understand their reasons for wanting or doing things.

A mixing game designed to show differences

How?
See examples on pages 139 - 141.

Red and blue realities

How?
1. Divide the group in half and call them blue group and red. Give red group a copy of a red role play and a red and blue summary sheet each, and blue group a copy of a blue role play and a red and blue summary sheet each.
2. Each red or blue group member fills in an individual red and blue summary sheet up to and including "and I feel ...."
3. Red group and blue group pair up. They are to make sure they say what they want, what their reasons are and how they are feeling but then they must also try to find out what the other person's point of view is. Agree a signal that they will use to show they have been successful.
4. A go-round to hear whether what they thought the other persons reasons were for behaving the way they did were true or not. Make the point that lots of problems are caused by guessing or assuming people's reasons for doing things instead of checking with them and listening to what they have to say.
5. Everyone can spend another minute writing down what their partner has said on their summary sheet and thinking what to suggest they could try to do about things.
6. Ask the pupils to remind you how to show someone with your body and voice that you are understanding them and you are willing to negotiate.

7. Now they can finish off, checking that they understand each other by summarising and saying, "You want..." "You feel..." and "You think..." to each other, and then making suggestions about what they could try.
8. Circle go-round to comment on what they and their partner did well and what would make it even better, also to share any solutions arrived at.
9. Pupils can repeat the exercise with a new partner omitting the summary sheets and relying on their memory or they can choose a new disagreement and a new partner for themselves and use the process again.

Steps 4 and 5. Creating solutions and agreeing ways forward

Young people who are accustomed to adult intervention and to being serviced by adults at home and at school can at first appear to be resourceless. This is not the case. By the time they reach this stage in the programme of activities with their peers and an enabling adult, they will have had ample opportunity to develop and demonstrate how creative and resourceful they are.

Brainstorming and evaluating

Why?
  To understand the difference between brainstorming and evaluating.
  To give practice at generating creative solutions - intrinsic parts of the mediation process.

Organisation:
  Circle Time.

Resources:
  Flip chart or big sheet of paper and pens.

How?
  1. Begin by explaining that a brainstorm is a way of creative thinking and that all suggestions are accepted without comment or evaluation.
  2. Begin with something simple such as brainstorming the uses of an orange e.g. to eat, to use pips to grow another plant, to use as a ball, to print with, to use as a weight, to use as a candle holder, to tie on the end of a piece of string to act as a pendulum, to adorn a carnival hat, etc..
  3. A task can be set, reducing litter in the school, making the lunchtime supervisor's job easier, and the pupils are asked to brainstorm strategies onto a large sheet of paper as a whole group or as several small groups.
  4. The teacher extends this activity as long as possible. It is useful to use such phrases as:

- In an ideal world...
- It doesn't have to make sense...
- Just write it all down...
- Try not to think about it too much at this stage...
- Imagine you had a magic wand...

5. The pupils are then asked to go back over what they have written and use a different pen to cross things out, change things or underline the best ideas. Ask them to be clear about why they are wanting to do some things and not others, can they give reasons to support why they think something would or would not work?

6. At the end the pupils are asked to use what they have written to create an action plan with clear points. Who will do what and when? How will they evaluate success? Do they need to create a contract?

Extensions:

Quick solutions

How?

Divide pupils into small groups. Give a series of problems and ask them to brainstorm quick solutions as fast as they can in one minute. Quickly hear each groups suggestion before moving on to the next problem.

The Disney Strategy

Walt Disney used this strategy to generate new possibilities and to sift, organise and evaluate them (Dilts, R. and Epstein, T. 1989).

How?

1. Put three mats or pieces of paper on the floor in the centre of the circle. Explain that the first one is for brainstorming possibilities, the second one is for thinking about how to put them into action and the third one is for noticing how they can be improved.

2. Pupils volunteer to 'walk through' a problem by stepping on each mat in turn. The rest of the group contribute to the activity indicated by the mat on which the pupil is standing. Problems can be whole-group ones, such as how to use their wet play time or individual ones such as how to help someone who is behind with their work.
3. The individual who asks for their problem to be used can choose to walk through the steps themselves or to nominate someone to do it on their behalf.
4. This need not be done as a whole-group activity, it could be done in pairs or triads, but it will need to be modelled first for the whole group.

Problem solving in the circle

Why?
To encourage collaborative approaches to resolving conflict.
To develop a sense of group responsibility and mutual aid.

Organisation:
Circle Time.

Note
Circle Time is not a therapy group , neither is it a substitute for one to one consultations with pupils experiencing problems. For all of the following activities it is important that pupils and teachers are clear about what is and is not appropriate as subject matter for problem solving. As a general guideline it may be useful to exclude anything concerned with private family life and to closely follow school procedures relating to child protection and the Children Act. (Department of Health 1991.)

Puppets

How?
1. Use puppets or mascots to introduce a problem that members of the class are experiencing. This will help to distance the problem and allow people to reflect on the issues and feelings involved without singling anybody out.
2. Having presented a short scenario and explained the problem attributed to the puppet, have a go-round where pupils say what they imagine the puppet is feeling.
3. Follow this with a go-round of suggestions of what the puppet could do or what we could offer to do to help them.
4. Summarise what has been said and where appropriate ask them to make links to what has been happening in the class.

Thinking hats

How?

1. Make/Collect or assemble 6 different colour hats or tokens. Each object symbolises a particular way of thinking about a problem as follows:
   - Grey = pessimist
   - Yellow = optimist
   - Red = about feelings
   - White = factual
   - Green = new growth, future possibilities
   - Blue = evaluation and bringing together all the other hats.
2. Get pupils to find a memory trick to help them to remember which colour/object means what.
3. Put the objects in the centre of the circle. Select each one in turn and encourage pupils to pass it round or pick it up if they want to make a contribution by thinking about the problem in the way symbolised by it. e.g. If they were talking about how to use wet playtimes and they wanted to talk about feeling cooped up or fed-up, they would use the red hat ; if they wanted to make a suggestion for a possible way forward , then they would use the green object.
4. The teacher can ensure that pupils have thought about a problem in a variety of ways by encouraging the use of all the hats. If pupils get stuck in a particular way of thinking e.g. if they become overly pessimistic, then the teacher can ask for contributions from people holding the yellow object.

Source: De Bono, E. (1985).

The four step process

How?

1. Explain the four steps. These are:
   - A volunteer pupil with a problem connected with school life, talks about it for as long as they need to.
   - A circle go-round in which pupils either summarise what they heard said or ask questions for clarification only. The pupil with the problem answers direct questions.
   - In the next go-round pupils say either, " ...name... what I think I might do in your situation is....................." or "What I could offer to do to help is.............." The pupil with the problem listens but doesn't need to respond.
   - After time for reflection the pupil with the problem feeds back to the group which suggestions and/or support s/he wishes to

act on.

2. Before they use the process pupils need to remind themselves and each other of the ground rules of Circle Time and to agree to:
    - avoid mentioning by name other pupils who may be involved in the problem
    - avoid gossiping about what is said in the circle
    - avoid saying "You should..." or "You ought......." or " Why didn't you?........."

3. It needs to be stressed that this process is about opening up a range of possibilities and not about making judgements or giving advice.

4. If a problem appears to be branching into areas that are inappropriate for school or for Circle Time the process should be diverted back into safe waters and followed up with individual consultation .

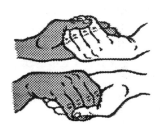

Conflict Questionnaire Sheet

Here are some examples of what different people think about conflicts and how they might act in a conflict situation. Answer the questionnaire with the example of a conflict you have chosen to focus on with your group in mind.

You can give a score from 1 to 5 according to how strongly each comment agrees (5) or disagrees (1) with your own usual thoughts or ways of dealing with the conflict you have in mind.

1 = disagree strongly, never the way I act.	4 = agree, usually the way I act.
2 = disagree, I hardly ever act that way.	5 = agree strongly, always the way I act.
3 = partly agree, sometimes the way I act.	

A ☐ I try not to get into an argument in the first place

B ☐ It's best to put your foot down and insist on getting your way

C ☐ You can always overcome enemies with kindness

D ☐ It's better to have half of something than nothing at all, so you should negotiate a way of sharing

E ☐ It's best to bring things out into the open and face them

F ☐ In a quarrel it is the person who stays silent first who is behaving the best

G ☐ It's alright to use force to get your way

H ☐ Saying things nicely softens people up

I ☐ If you do something for me I'll do something for you

J ☐ You should set out to know what the other persons side is , so that you know the truth

K ☐ It's better to stay clear of any fighting

L ☐ You can tell you've won properly when the other person runs away

M ☐ If people would just speak politely to each other then everything would be fine

135

N ☐ It's alright to argue as long as you both get the chance to put your point across and both get something out of it

O ☐ Frankness and honesty is the only way to sort things out

P ☐ It's best to avoid people who give you hassle

Q ☐ It's best to act like you're right and they are wrong

R ☐ It doesn't cost you anything to say something positive & it usually helps

S ☐ It's better for both people to give in and meet each other half way

T ☐ It's better to keep digging until you understand what they're getting at

U ☐ Nothing is so important that you should fight about it

V ☐ You should stand your ground to make them give in

W ☐ A gentle word will always get the better of an angry person

X ☐ You can usually find a fair swap to sort things out

Y ☐ You can't act as if only one of you is right, you need to get their side

Z ☐ Just keep out of arguments they only cause you grief

Aa ☐ If you are arguing for something you think is best you try to make the other person do what you think is best

Bb ☐ If someone says or does something hard it's better to reply softly

Cc ☐ Getting half of what you want is better than not getting anything at all

Dd ☐ You don't know all the answers. It's better to know why it matters to the other person

Ee ☐ The best way to handle conflicts is to avoid them

Ff ☐ Some people are just born leaders. They always know the best thing to do

Gg ☐ You can have harmony if you both offer to do something for each other

Hh ☐ If you both give something to each other it will help mend things be tween you

Ii ☐ It's best to say, "Let's sort this out together now."

Conflict questionnaire answer sheet

Fill in your responses in one of the columns on this sheet. Find the letter of the question (A , B, Aa Gg Hh etc.) in one of the columns below and write next to it your score.

There are no right or wrong ways of answering the comments. Whatever you put will be right for you.

Style 1	Style 2	Style 3	Style 4	Style 5
A..........	B.........	C........	D........	E........
F........	G.......	H........	I.........	J.........
K........	L.......	M........	N........	O........
P........	Q.......	R.........	S........	T........
U.........	V.......	W........	X.........	Y.........
Z.........	Aa......	Bb......	Cc......	Dd.......
Ee......	Ff.......	Gg......	Hh......	Ii.........
Total [ ]	Total [ ]	Total [ ]	Total [ ]	Total [ ]

Each of the columns represents a different way of responding to conflict, what we can call a conflict style. The higher the score for each column, the more comfortable you are with that particular way of handling conflicts or conflict style. The lower the score the less you tend to use that style. Have a look and see if your scores tell you anything you didn't already know.

This is what the different styles can be called....

     ⇒   1. Withdrawing
     ⇒   2. Forcing
     ⇒   3. Smoothing
     ⇒   4. Compromising
     ⇒   5. Confronting.

All of the styles have their particular uses. There are no good or bad styles. Only good styles that sometimes get used in the wrong situations. For example, if you felt that something unsafe or totally wrong was about to happen, you wouldn't use either compromising or smoothing as a first choice, you would need to weigh up the situation and make a choice between withdrawal (especially if your safety was at stake) confronting (if you needed to know what was going on) or forcing (if you needed to protect your rights or someone else's right).

What matters is that you know which style suits particular situations best and that you try not to get stuck with only one style of responding.

Prompt sheet

Say what happened (using facts but not opinions)..............

Say how you feel about it................

Say why you are feeling that way..................

Say politely and clearly what you would like to see happen.............................

Red role play slip 1.

You find the weather very hot because you are trying to make ice-cream in the shape of a ghost for a ghost party and it keeps melting.

You open the windows to cool it down.

Blue person closes all the windows and lights the fire!

You put the fire out and open the windows to cool the ice-cream.

Blue person closes them and lights the fire again.

- ◆ What do you need?
- ◆ Why do you need it?
- ◆ Why do you think blue person is doing these things?
- ◆ How do you feel:
    - about your ice-cream?
    - about blue person?

Blue role play slip 1.

You find the weather very cold because you've just come home from crossing the desert, you only have thin clothes to wear and you are starting to get a sore throat.

Red person opens all the windows and lets the cold air in.

You close them and light the fire.

Red person puts the fire out and opens the windows again.

- ◆ What do you need?
- ◆ Why do you need it?
- ◆ Why do you think red person is doing these things?
- ◆ How do you feel:
    - about being so cold and having a sore throat?
    - about red person?

Red role play slip 2.

You've just been on a cross country and you've come in tired and boiling hot.

You need to let some fresh air into the classroom, so you open the windows.

Blue person gets up and closes them.

After a while you open them again.

Soon after Blue person closes them all again.

- ♦ What do you need?
- ♦ Why do you need it?
- ♦ What do you feel?
- ♦ Why do you think blue person is doing these things?
- ♦ What do you feel about the blue person at the moment?

Blue role play slip 2.

You've just been doing swimming in P.E. The water was freezing and your hair is still wet. You left your jumper in the changing rooms. You're feeling shivery and you can feel a cold coming.

Red person opens all the windows.

You get up and close them.

After a bit they get up and open them again.

- ♦ What do you need?
- ♦ Why do you need it?
- ♦ What do you feel?
- ♦ Why do you think red person is doing these things?
- ♦ What do you feel about the red person at the moment?

Red and Blue Summary Sheet

I want ....

because ....

and I feel ....

you want ....

because...

you feel ....

and you think ....

we could try ....

Red and Blue Summary Sheet

I want ....

because ....

and I feel ....

you want ....

because...

you feel ....

and you think ....

we could try ....

Chapter 9
Peer Mediation

If a class has worked through the skills and some of the activities in this book, then peer mediation will be the icing on the cake, and will provide genuine practice of the skills they will have acquired. As discussed elsewhere, setting up a **Peer Mediation** intervention is different in each school. (Robinson and Stacey 1997)

Although all pupils may have had a go at role-playing being a mediator, ultimately a group of pupils will need to be chosen to offer a service for their peers. Sometimes they are nominated by their peers, sometimes they nominate themselves, and sometimes staff will choose the pupils who they think would make the best mediators. An ideal group size is twelve to sixteen, and a team of mediators can either be taken from one year group or from across all year groups with older pupils.

It is important for the team of mediators to be off timetable together for between one and three days depending on how much listening and mediation practice they have had with the rest of their class. An intensive period of time such as this allows for team building and proper rehearsal of counselling skills but more importantly it allows young people the opportunity to develop their own guidelines for effective practice and to design their own service. Included in this training will be the members of staff who are to support the peer mediators throughout the year, lunchtime supervisors and any other adults or ancillary staff offering their support. (Education Social Workers, School Nurse, Secretarial staff, parents, governors, home/school liaison workers etc.)

Decisions need to made, not only about what sort of problems are appropriate for pupil mediators to deal with, how pupils access the service and whether referral is through adults, but also the finer details of rota and responsibilities for running the scheme from day to day. In many models the service takes place at lunchtime four times a week. Some choose to withdraw into a quiet room or private corner, whilst other services operate out in play areas at a designated spot. We have become familiar with many mediation trees, benches and gates! The level of publicity and support from staff can determine whether a mediation service will stand or fall. In the schools where the services have been most successful the staff, including the lunchtime supervisors, have had at least one in-service training session after school, dedicated to peer mediation, and ideally a full training day. One of the best examples of this was when the pupil mediators themselves came in on a training day and taught the whole staff mediation skills. If staff have full awareness of what the process involves they are then able to make full use of voluntary referral slips which can be kept in registration folders.

Other successful initiatives have ensured that a high profile is maintained throughout the year. Pupils themselves are in a best position to know how to market and advertise their service amongst their peers, but will benefit from a partnership with I.T. Media Studies, Art, Drama and Business Education Partnership etc. Here is an opportunity to use photographs, video footage, posters and presentations, Parents and Governors meetings, word of mouth strategies (e.g. undertaking to tell ten people each who are in turn asked to tell ten other people) newsletters and input into P.S.E. or Circle Time in other classes, to launch the service and maintain a high profile. Many peer mediation schemes give themselves a clear identity, choosing names (Trouble Busters, Helping Hands, Untanglers) logos, slogans ('Release the peace and be strong') and forms of identification such as baseball caps, badges and sweatshirts which allow them to be easily identified when on duty.

Although peer mediators need to have ownership of their service and make the decisions and choices about the way in which the service runs, they need regular adult support and supervision. This varies according to the age of the pupils involved, but all will need a weekly team meeting to debrief, to share experiences and to keep up a regular programme of review and development.
The burden entailed in providing regular support for the mediators will be lessened if it is a shared responsibility between more than one member of staff, and if the staff members involved feel confident in their own mediation skills and in the level of expertise they can bring to support sessions with the pupil team.

It is rare for any service to work perfectly from the word go. Even the most established schemes (3 or 4 years) need modifying or altering completely as the needs of the users change over time. Some schools in Birmingham experience a falling-off in the use of peer mediators as the curriculum work takes root and mediation becomes a familiar enough process for pupils to sort problems out early on, between themselves, without recourse to peer mediators. There will never be a time when conflict between pupils vanishes altogether, but peer mediators may eventually need to change the focus of their service to one, for example, where they promote positive play at Primary level or become a source of information and referral at Secondary level.

The usual age at which pupils are trained to become peer mediators is at top Junior (10-11 years old) or in any Secondary year. There is however one example in Birmingham of top Infant children (7 year olds) being trained to mediate successfully in a rudimentary way for their peers. Seven year olds are able to mediate in the sense that they can support two people who are in disagreement to hear each others feelings and agree what to do for the best. Junior peer mediators are well able to provide a neutral, non-judgmental service. Success depends on the curriculum work already in place and the school's support for their emerging independence. Ten and eleven year old mediators can help disputants to understand what the problem is about, appreciate each others point of view and choose a way forward that will change things for the good of both.

All age groups at Secondary phase can mediate successfully for their peers. With increasing age and maturity comes increasing perception and sophistication, and the ability to reach underlying issues as well as to identify unexpressed needs. A mediation between primary pupils may be over in a matter of minutes. Older pupils may need recourse to several sessions of mediation before reaching a resolution. Mediation between adults often averages six hours in total. The process of mediation, however, is broadly similar no matter what the context of the conflict is, or the ages of those involved. For easy assimilation the process is taught as a series of steps, although in reality the steps are often revisited in a cyclical fashion which soon becomes an intuitive process for the mediators.

Infant Mediation

Beginners and infants can become mediators provided that they have been following the programmes outlined earlier in this book or other similar programmes from elsewhere. Clearly, they can use the process as disputants, with older or more experienced children mediating, relatively early on in their prosocial skills development work.

The skills that they will need in order to be mediators at this level are:
- Memory
- Impartiality
- Listening
- Repeating
- Assertiveness
- Brainstorming.

These skills will initially be developed by using the activities from the relevant sections in this book. The mediation work will allow the pupils to consolidate their skills in role-play and then real life situations. The process at infant level tends to be very short (1 to 5 minutes) and ritualised. What the disputants often want is to be heard, and some help to think of quick solutions.

The Infant Mediation Process
1. Remember to be fair to both of them and not to tell anyone off.
2. Say the rules. "Please talk one at a time. Please don't call each other names."
3. Ask them what the problem is and how they are feeling, one at a time.
4. Repeat what each person said after they have said it.
5. Ask each of them to tell you how the other is feeling.
6. Make a list with them of things that they could do to sort out problem.
7. Help them to choose what they are going to do.

Training Infant Mediators

The best way to teach this process to infants is to model it in real life disputes as often as possible. A demonstration by you of the process with two of the pupils role playing a dispute and the rest of them watching is a good way to present the seven steps.

They can be helped to remember the steps by practising them a few at a time over a number short sessions before trying them all together, and they can also help you to devise a series of symbols (a heart for asking about feelings, a parrot for repeating etc.) to be displayed on the classroom walls whilst they are practising.

One group of year two pupils taught us the value of using hand signals as memory hooks. They devised a hand signal for each step and made them into a sequence which they did as they went through the process.

Junior and Lower Secondary Mediation

At this level, which is usually appropriate for juniors and lower secondary, the process is more or less the process that is used in the community by adults.

The process has been written as a worksheet that can be given to children to help them to remember what to do next. It is printed on page 160.

Training Junior/Lower Secondary Mediators

The following lists, pages 146 and 147, were produced by a group of Birmingham teachers in November 1996, as a way of assessing the skills that pupils would need in order to participate in the mediation process both as disputants and as mediators. They provide teachers with a summary of the skills to be learned, at least partially, before pupils will be able to mediate for each other and use the process to resolve their disputes. Clearly the process of peer mediation will serve to build on and enhance these skills, but, as will be clear by now, peer mediation will fail if it is done without some prior skills-building work with all pupils.

The best way to teach this process to pupils is to give them a demonstration by asking two of them to role play a dispute with you or a professional mediator mediating, or to show a video of a mediation (Contact Catalyst Consultancy for information about videos). This can be followed by a discussion about what you did.

The Disputants

Step One Introduction and Ground Rules

- Self control
- Impulse control
- Understanding of what the rules mean and why they are important

Step Two Problem and Feelings

- Self expression including the ability to narrate and describe facts and events, and to express feelings
- Language and Vocabulary
- Confidence
- Honesty
- Listening
- Patience

Step Three Acknowledging the other person's point of view

- Awareness of the existence of different perspectives
- Empathy
- The ability to affirm another person

Step Four Brainstorming Solutions

- Brainstorming
- Sharing
- Being positive and creative

Step Five Agreeing a Solution

- Compromising
- Negotiating
- Valuing other's contributions
- Willingness to try new things
- Problem-solving

The Mediators

Step One Introduction and Ground Rules

- Welcoming, friendly manner
- Memory
- Confidence
- Assertiveness
- Tact

Step Two Problem and Feelings

- Memory
- Listening
- Awareness of body language
- Self control and ability to stay calm
- Awareness of when and how to step in to reinforce ground rules
- Summarising
- Asking open questions for clarification and to encourage disputants to speak

Step Three Acknowledging the other person's point of view

- Summarising feelings and needs
- Range of techniques for encouraging empathy
- Ability to use neutral language and tone of voice

Step Four Brainstorming Solutions

- Friendly manner
- Ability to encourage offers
- Positive attitude
- Brainstorming

Step Five Agreeing a Solution

- Listening
- Summarising
- Negotiating
- Positive affirming attitude

Before the pupils attempt the process they will need to be reminded of the basic listening skills work that they have done. They need to be reminded to listen with acceptance, to summarise accurately without repeating everything that was said, to listen sensitively for feelings and to reflect them back, and to avoid making judgments or offering advice.

Role-plays work best if the pupils have been well prepared for them. They will need some time to think around the situation and get into role. Clearly both disputants will need to agree in advance what the problem is and exactly what happened. The mediators (always working in pairs) will also need some time to write down in their own words the kinds of things they would like to say during the mediation.

They may well need to be reminded to be gentle with each other when role-playing disputants as they often dig their heels in and forget that they are supposed to have come to the mediators to ask for help.

We have found the following worksheets, pages 160 - 164, to be useful in helping to prepare pupils for role-plays. We have also included a series of conflict situations that pupils helped us to brainstorm, although it may be better for each class to brainstorm their own to ensure authenticity and relevance.

Setting up the Service

When the mediators are quite comfortable with the mediation process, they can begin to design their service. We have included here Alston Junior School Mediators handbook as an example of what children can produce with some support. It is specific to their school and not to be taken as the only way of providing a service, but it is comprehensive and shows how the children have been encouraged to consider a wide range of issues.

The Suggestions for a Mediation Service section is a write-up of an initial brainstorm, and includes some impractical suggestions (mediate in the staffroom at breaktimes!) alongside some very good suggestions.

The Mediators Help Booklet was designed both to make them aware of situations when they would and would not mediate, and to provide an information booklet for staff, lunchtime supervisors, governors and parents.

The questions and answers section was the result of pupils writing onto sheets of paper the 'What if's' that they could think of in connection with their service. They worked in groups and circulated the 'What if's' amongst the groups so that they could write suggestions for each other onto the pieces of paper. In this way they were answering their own concerns and building on the sense of team that was already beginning to emerge. We were able to support them with clear boundaries about what they would and would not be expected to mediate, and by giving them information when they asked for it about schemes in other schools.

Alston Junior School Mediators

Suggestions for a Mediation service.
- Have Badge.
- Mediate in.. . Playground, staffroom, hall, music room, science room, art room.
- Advertise with a poster with photos on and times available.
- Take an assembly.
- Do it at playtimes.
- We may need to ask a teacher for extra time to finish a mediation.
- Have a rota and a timetable.

Mediators on duty in the playground escort people in to be mediated or give them a card or token to show that they have had permission (teachers could give cards too).

Some guidelines for good practice

The Mediators help booklet.
1. Mediators are there to help people who want helping. They can't make people come to mediation if they don't want to.
2. You would never mediate a fight or bad argument while it was going on.
3. Mediators do not mediate disagreements when they are to do with family things.
4. They do not mediate things which are against the law or are to do with school rules or property. (like stealing, using a weapon or going where you shouldn't go.)
5. They do not mediate violent things or things where people have been attacked.
6. Mediators do not keep bad secrets. They keep things private and don't gossip, but they do talk to their mediation teacher (Ms Moon) about the things they have been mediating.
7. If they heard something that was dangerous to another person then they would tell their teacher straight away.
8. If they have to stop a mediation because of something that has happened, then they would tell their mediation teacher.
9. Mediators can mediate things like...

- being left out
- or called names
- or if your friend falls out with you
- or if you feel something isn't fair.

10. They can mediate when.. .
    - people feel people are picking on them
    - or teasing them
    - and if someone has done something to make you feel un happy or angry.

11. They can also help people to.. .
    - stop arguing about something
    - or to find a way of both agreeing to do something to make it better in the future.

12. Mediators don't tell people what to do.

13. They help people to decide what to do for themselves.

14. Mediators don't take sides and don't say who is right or who is wrong. They listen to both people.

15. Mediators help people to stick to the rules by reminding them..
    - not to butt in
    - not to swear at the other person
    - or call them names
    - and not to keep blaming the other person.

16. They need to...
    - wait their turn to talk
    - say what the problem is for them
    - and call the other person by their proper name.

If disputants keep on breaking the rules then the mediator can't help them and the mediation will have to stop.

Questions

Here are some questions and answers to do with mediating.

What if one of the people wouldn't speak?

Ask if they want a friend to speak for them or get someone to talk their language.

What if they both won't speak?

Well you could start the talking by saying what you guess the problem is. If they still won't talk then you should say that you can't help them unless they help you by saying something.

What if they wouldn't stop butting in?

If they start getting cheeky, then after you have reminded them once not to, then you have to stop the mediation until they can keep the rule about listening and not butting in.

What if they wouldn't agree to the rules?
Then you can't do a mediation.

What if you have a fight or a bad argument in the mediation?
Stop the mediation and get a grown up.

What if a problem is with a teacher and someone?
You would have to talk to your mediation teacher, Ms. Moon or Ms. Sneddon or someone.

What if it is your brother or someone in your family that wants mediating?
Get somebody else to do the mediation.

What if YOU need mediating?
Just go to the mediators, they will help you.

What if a mediator falls out with another mediator in the mediation?
Well you have to really say before the mediation which bits you are going to do and if you are telling the other mediator that they have missed a bit out or something then you can do it politely and kindly so they don't get cross.

What if the mediation doesn't work?
Mediation doesn't work all the time. You could ask if they want to come back and try again another time. Sometimes you might think that it hasn't worked because they don't want to be friends, but it has worked if they are both agreeing not to be friends for the moment and to keep away from each other for example.

What if someone bursts out crying?
Let him or her cry a bit and be kind. Don't say "Don't cry." You could say, "We can see you're really upset.. Have a tissue." Something like that.

What if the problem is about something at home?
Stop the mediation and say that it would be better to get Ms. Moon or another teacher they like to talk to about it. You can't mediate about home problems.

What if we run out of mediators for all the problems?
You could make a list of who is waiting and give them different times to come back.

What if the person being mediated has got a bad temper?
You could try to calm him or her by being calm. They might need to come back

when they don't feel so angry, or to count to 5 or 10 before they say things. But if it is breaking the rules then stop the mediation.

What if the person starts using violence?
Stop the mediation and get your teacher.

What if the problem is personal?
If it's very private talk to a teacher don't mediate. They might be just shy or something, so you could ask what kind of person they would like to be mediated by.

What if the problem is a really bad one about knives?
Stop the mediation. Get your teacher.

What if your best friend wants you to be their mediator?
Say you can't be on their side so they may as well have someone else to be their mediator.

What if you're stuck what to do next?
Have a break and ask your mediation teacher or another mediator to help.

Help each other
and
Be proud of yourself.

Upper Secondary Mediation

Many of the activities and worksheets from the intermediate section are relevant with older pupils. Older pupils are able, however, to deal with more complex issues and to see connections and underlying tensions more clearly.

Wherever we have supported older pupils (years 9-11) to provide a mediation service, they have also wanted to offer a peer counselling service. This has involved the development of basic counselling skills. These are:

- Helping a 'client' to feel comfortable enough to speak to them about problems or concerns.
- Open and relaxed body language.
- Good questioning techniques.

- Awareness of underlying feelings and issues.
- Summarising skills.
- Non-judgmental acceptance of the client.
- Awareness that the counselling role is not about giving advice or getting the client to do things your way.

Teaching Basic Counselling

<u>Why?</u>
To promote peer support.

<u>How?</u>
1. Brainstorm the difference in the way a reporter listens and the way a counsellor listens. It should emerge that a reporter listens for him/herself, in order to extract information from someone, whereas a counsellor listens mainly for the benefit of the person who is talking, to help them to be clear about what their problem is and what they can do about it.

Body Language and Physical Environment
2. Reflect back on what they learnt about body language during the thirty second listening exercise (Speaking and listening at Intermediate level).
3. Give out the worksheet on body language, page 165.

Questioning Techniques
4. Explain the difference between open and closed questions. Closed questions can usually be answered by a simple yes, no, don't know or a brief fact, and can create a silence. They are useful to illicit specific information and to verify when and where things happened. Open questions encourage the client to talk more freely and begin with words like What and How or phrases such as "tell me more about that....." They leave the client free to answer in a variety of ways and to explore their thoughts and feelings more thoroughly.
5. Give out questioning worksheet, page 166.
6. Give out Open Questions worksheet to consolidate open questions activities, page 167.

Positions, interests and needs
7. Discuss the fact that in a conflict situation people will often state a position, e.g. "I never want to see my friend again." A good counsellor will help to identify the interests and needs that lie underneath this statement., e.g. "I am upset because my friend wouldn't play with me."

There is a well known sequence of needs developed by Gustav Maslow (1968), and it is often useful to consider which of these basis needs has not been met in the situation in which the client or disputant finds him or herself.

Write the needs randomly on the board and ask pupils to decide in small groups a sequence where the most basic need is at the bottom and so on. When they have done this write them up in the right order (according to Maslow!) as follows:

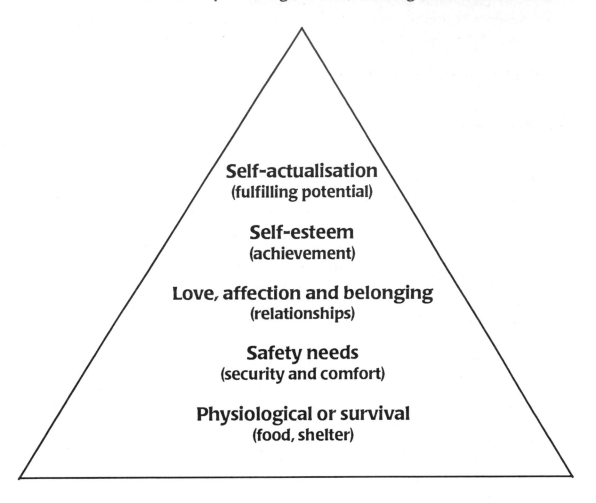

Self-actualisation
(fulfilling potential)

Self-esteem
(achievement)

Love, affection and belonging
(relationships)

Safety needs
(security and comfort)

Physiological or survival
(food, shelter)

8. To consolidate this, ask pupils in pairs to take it in turns to choose a need and present it as an imaginary problem. Their partner uses their counselling skills to find out about the problem and the underlying need.

The mediation process at Upper Secondary level

The following process is presented as a flow-diagram to indicate the often cyclical nature of mediations as the problems become more sophisticated. The added dimension at this level is the part in the process where the mediators summarise the main issues and needs.

The best way of training pupils to use this model is to use their ideas of common conflict situations in school to create a series of role-play situations. They can then use these situations in groups of four (two disputants and two mediators) to gain practice.

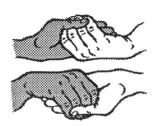

The mediation Process

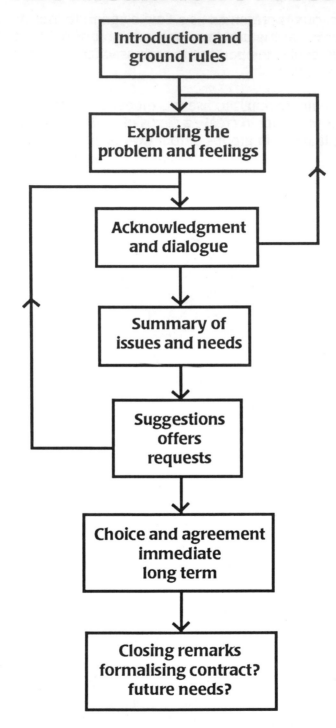

Introduction and ground rules

Exploring the problem and feelings

Acknowledgment and dialogue

Summary of issues and needs

Suggestions offers requests

Choice and agreement immediate long term

Closing remarks formalising contract? future needs?

And finally...............

We believe, from our experience of developing peer mediation services in countless schools, that it really works. We have left the final words for the educationalists, teachers and pupils who are using it as part of their everyday lives.

One characteristic of peer-mediation training is the way it seems to improve a school's ethos and raise teacher-expectations. This was made evident by a short questionnaire-based case-study of the core group of Birmingham schools where peer-mediation has been established, comparing the expressed views of teachers in these schools with those of the larger number of pupils actually trained as mediators. This study was carried out in 1995, 1996 (details from Hilary Stacey, at Nene College, Northampton).

Briefly, teachers who hope for improvements in pupil self-esteem and general social competence strongly verify that such hopes are achieved. Especially, they report "massive" rises in self-esteem amongst pupils trained as mediators. This observation is confirmed by pupils themselves, in both primary and secondary schools. In interview, a fourteen year old said of her mediation work: "It gives you confidence. I mean.. . if I hadn't done that training, I don't think I could have stood out and made that opening speech" (this youngster had opened a Children's Conference with some aplomb). A younger pupil affirmed: "I've got more confidence.. . It's really good, like, listening to people.. . If you do something good like this.. . you know, you earn respect". It isn't that common for pupils to become so aware of their own, improving social skills.

What is also deduced strongly from the interview data gathered during this study is the way these youngsters are able to discuss moral issues in a sophisticated and mature manner. Peer-mediation training is geared to helping children mediate between those engaged in a quarrel. To do this, they are forced to become conscious both of the subtleties of disagreement possible between human beings and the difference between fair and unfair solutions. The training programme therefore shows itself to be not only a way of improving a school's behaviour-management policy but a way of morally educating the young. This is not always the case with the behavioural-improvement strategies currently being used in schools.
Dr. Peter Silcock, Senior Lecturer, Nene College, Northampton.

Mediation began as an aspect of school life, a taught element, and has become something which they use as part of their everyday lives, as useful as language and maths. Their skills at whatever level, have extended into their homes and lives outside school.
Sarah Hodgson. Behaviour Coordinator. Adderley J.I. School Birmingham.

We were looking for ways to further enhance our behaviour policy when we first became involved with mediation. Our sense of self worth affects every aspect of our lives. I believe it is vital therefore, that we provide our children with the opportunities to develop high self esteem, leading to a transfer of power base and responsibility.

The processes involved in Mediation seemed just what we were looking for. In fact I was far more interested in affirmation, listening, communicating and cooperation than in actually ending up with peer mediation in school. Nevertheless we decided that we would introduce peer mediation. I'm so glad we did. Our first mediators were brilliant. It was wonderful to watch them grow in confidence as the scheme got underway and was successful. Our third group of mediators has just started. The children never fail to amaze us. They get better every year.
There is a down side however, if mediation works well. The mediators get bored, as they've nothing to do! We're going to train them as playleaders this year so that they have something to do when all the problems are solved.

The whole process of mediation has made a huge difference in our school. We find it almost impossible to say exactly why it has worked so well. It is a combination of many things. Perhaps the most important is that we did it as a whole school.

I can't imagine our school without mediation. We feel really proud of what our children have achieved using the processes of mediation.
Judith Jones. Headteacher Adderley Primary School Birmingham.

The Peer Mediation Process has proved to be a valuable tool since it began seven months ago. The skills taught to all of the pupils have helped to create a positive and pleasant atmosphere within classrooms and around the school. The chosen Mediators themselves have grown in stature, assuming responsibility for operating the scheme. Their mature approach has been appreciated by disputants and their success has certainly eased my pastoral workload.
Niger Cassley. Head of year 7. Barley Green Secondary School Birmingham.

" I think it's a very good idea. It's helped me to cooperate with my friends more and more, and people trust on me more and I really like that."
" I like mediating because I want our school to be a very nice and friendly place and everyone cooperating together."
" It makes me feel very confident with myself and proud with myself as

well."

"Mediation has certainly helped the pupils to get along with each other better."

"It is good to see pupils get into the habit and feel confident to share concerns in front of the mediators."

"Most problems are sorted out in a matter of minutes, occasionally there are difficult problems that can take a few sessions to sort out, but usually agreement is the end product."

"We think everyone should go to mediation about their problems because it will mean that in the future school will be a happier place to be."

"I really enjoy the responsibility of listening to others and I take my role as mediator very seriously."

"The training is pretty good. It's helped me. I've found a lot of skills I never knew I had."

"I feel good (about being a mediator) because I used to have problems as well and I couldn't talk to no- one."

"I think it's going well. They (younger pupils) do seem to be opening up more now. They seem to trust you more as well."

"With teachers yeh?... they usually shout at you right?...or blame you.. .see? but with the mediators right? they don't blame you, they don't take sides. They're hard on the problem but soft on the people see?"

"It makes you feel good inside to know that you have helped somebody else who needs your help."

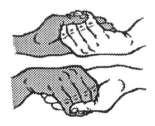

Mediation

Step One

The mediator's promises:
- She/he will not take sides
- She/he will not offer any solutions
- She/he will not tell anyone else about what happens in the mediation unless she/he is seriously worried about someone's safety

The mediator's rules.
Ask them:
- To talk one at a time and not to interrupt each other
- To speak with respect and not to call each other names
- To try to talk about the problem from their own point of view and not blame or accuse the other person

Step Two
- Ask each one in turn what the **problem** is and how she/he **feels**
- **Repeat** what you have heard each one say

Step Three
- Ask each one if she/he can **acknowledge** other one's **feelings**

Step Four
- Ask them to offer **suggestions** about how they can sort things out

Step Five

- Ask them to agree a **solution** and ask if they need to meet again to see how they are getting on
- At all times mediators need to be positive. They should try to:
- Smile
- Thank people for coming
- Be calm
- Thank people for being patient
- Thank people for being helpful

What's The Problem?

What's your name?

How old are you?

What class are you in?

How many friends have you got?

What do you usually like to do at breaktime?

What's special or different about you?

What is your problem?

Where is it happening?

When is it happening?

How long has it been going on for?

Who have you talked to about it?

How are you feeling about your problem?

What has made you come to mediation?

What do you not want to happen?

What do you want to happen?

What would you be prepared to do to sort it out?

Mediators Prompt Sheet

What can you say at the beginning to welcome them and help them to relax?

How will you say your promises and their rules?

How will you decide who to ask to go first?

What will you say if one of them keeps breaking the rules?

What will you say if one of them is shy or sulking and won't say very much?

What will you say if one of them doesn't know how they are feeling?

What will you say if one of them says that they don't care about the problem?

What will you say just before you repeat what each person said?

What will you say if one of them can't acknowledge the other person's feelings?

What will you say if they get stuck and can't think of how they could sort it out?

What will you say to help them decide what they are going to do?

What will you say at the end of the mediation?

Role Plays

A. (Sahida) Wasim pushed in front of you when you were lining up and then swore at you when you tried to stop him. You told the teacher and he is now in trouble. He wants you to go to mediation with him to sort it out and you want to get it sorted as well.

B. (Wasim) Sahida is always at the front when you are lining up. When you pushed to the front the other day she tried to stop you. When you swore at her she told the teacher and now you are in trouble. The teacher says that if you can sort this out through mediation then she will be very pleased with you, and you want to get it sorted out.

A. (Baljinder) Today at breaktime Selma came up and asked you if she could have one of your crisps. She knew that you had two packets because you had one in your pocket from yesterday. When you said "no" she took the crisps from your pocket and started to run off with them. You shouted a bad name after her, and you still want your crisps back. Maybe the mediators could help.

B. (Selma) Today at breaktime you were starving because you didn't have any breakfast and you forgot to get some crisps. You knew that Baljinder had some left over from yesterday, so you asked her if you could have one of her crisps. She was mean and said "no" so you took her crisps from her pocket and ran off. You haven't eaten them, you just wanted to teach her a lesson. She called you a bad name, and now you are even more cross with her. Maybe the mediators could help.

A. (Sonya) You are best friends with Sam but when you were away from school for a week, Sam started to play with Sarah. You like Sarah, but you wish that you and Sam could play with each other on your own sometimes. Yesterday Sarah got cross because you asked her to let you play on your own with Sam for a bit. Now she has started to say horrible things about your mum to the other girls in your class. Sam says that she wishes that you and Sarah could be friends so you have said that you will ask for the help of the mediators.

B. (Sarah) When Sonya was away from school for a week you got really friendly with her best friend, Sam. You like Sam, and now that Sonya is back, you want to keep playing with her. Sonya seems moody when you are all playing together, and yesterday she told you to leave her and Sam alone for a bit. You don't see what gives her the right to tell you what to do. You have started to spread rumours about her mum to get your own back. Sam wishes that you and Sonya could be friends so you have said that you will ask for the help of the mediators.

A. (Andrew) You want to play football at dinnertime, but no-one will let you play in their team. The other day you got so fed up that you kicked the ball over the school fence. John, whose ball it is, is saying that he will fight you after school if you don't get it back for him. You want to sort it out through mediation.

B. (John) Andrew keeps wanting to play with you and your football at dinnertimes, but he is always late coming back to school and you are usually in the middle of a game. The other day he got so fed up that he kicked your ball over the fence. You want your ball back and you will fight him after school unless he gets it for you. You want to try mediation.

Body Language

Chair
At 90 degrees to the client, not directly facing them. Same height

Posture
Relaxed, open, not leaning too far forward or back

Arms
Loose, uncrossed

Hands
Not fidgeting, open, not in a fist. Avoid finger wagging or stabbing the air to make a point

Legs
Not crossed, feet on the floor

Eyes
Focusing on the client in a warm, interested, natural way

Head
Nod to convey agreement and give encouragement. Head on one side can signal empathy

Voice
Calm, clear with a warm tone

Questioning worksheet

Can you rephrase these closed questions as open questions?

1. Did the exam go well?

2. Do you hate school?

3. Are you getting on O.K. with your friends?

4. Do you have a good social life?

5. Do you find your work difficult?

6. Who started it?

7. When did you find out about it?

8. Are you feeling angry?

9. Do you want to be friends?

10. So, your teacher is annoyed about that?

Open Questions

Open questions can explore a problem more fully
- Tell me about that........
- Describe.................
- In what way.............
- Give me an example...................

Open questions can also be used to ask about feelings
- How did you feel when........
- What did you feel about......
- What are your feelings now...........

Open questions can be used to ask about what a client did and what their opinions are
- What did you do when......?
- And after that?
- What do you think about........?

Questions to avoid

1. Leading questions. This can be an undercover way of trying to influence the client.
    - You would agree with me on that.... wouldn't you?
    - Do you think that you did that because you were upset?
    - Would it have been better if............do you think?

2. Multi-choice questions. These are like closed questions. e.g.
    - Would you prefer to do.. ...or.....?

3. Multiple questions. Asking several questions together without waiting for a response. The client will generally answer the easiest question only

4. Asking a question and answering it yourself.
    - Why do you think she did that? Maybe because she was depressed?

5. Poorly timed questions. Especially ones which interrupt the client or stop them from expressing an emotion

Bibliography

Acland, A.F. (1990) A Sudden Outbreak of Common Sense: Managing Conflict through Mediation. Hutchinson Business Books.

Aronson, E., Bridgeman, D.L. and Geffner, R. (1978) The effects of a cooperative classroom structure on student behaviour and attitudes. In Bar-Tal, D. and Saxe, L.(eds) Social Psychology of Education. Wiley. New York.

Bliss, T., Robinson, G. and Maines, B. (1995) Coming Round to Circle Time. Lucky Duck Publishing.

Bliss, T., Robinson, G. and Maines, B. (1995) Developing Circle Time. Lucky Duck Publishing.

Bliss, T. and Tetley, J. (1993) Circle Time. Lucky Duck Publishing.

Clark A. C., and Walberg, H.J. (1968)   The influence of massive rewards on reading achievement in potential urban school drop outs. American Educational Reseach Journal. Vol. 5. No. 3.

Crum, T. (1987) The Magic of Conflict. Touchstone, New York.

Curle, A. (1987) True Justice: Quaker Peace Makers and Peace Making. Quaker Home Service, London.

Curry, M. and Bromfield, C. (1994) Personal and Social Education for Primary Schools through Circle Time. NASEN.

De Bono, E. (1985) Conflicts : A better way to resolve them. Penguin.

Department of Health (1991) The Children Act 1989. London H.M.S.O.

Dickson, A. (1989) A Woman in Her Own Right. Quartet.

Dilts, R. and Epstein, T. (1989) NLP in Training Groups, Dynamic Learning Publications.

Eisenberg, N. and Mussen, P.H. (1989) The Roots of Pro-social Behaviour in Children. Cambridge University Press.

Fine, N. and Macbeth, F. (1990) Playing with Fire. Training for the creative use of conflict. Youth Work Press

Goleman, D. (1996) Emotional Intelligence. Bloomsbury, London.

Harris, T. A. (1973) I'm OK, You're OK. Pan. London.

Hartley, R.L. (1986) Imagine you're clever. Journal of Child Psychology and Psychiatry. Vol.27. No. 3.

Holloway, J. (1994) Rainbow of Words. NASEN.

Johnson, D. W. and Johnson, R. T. (1991) Teaching Students to be Peacemakers. Interactive Book Company. Minnesota.

Kohlberg, L. (1975) The cognitive - developmental approach to moral education. Phi Delta Kappa, June.

Kohlberg, L. and Higgins, A. (1987) School Democracy and Social Interaction. In Kurtines, W.M. and Gewirtz, J.L. (Eds) Moral Development through Social Interaction. Wiley-Interscience. New York.

Kreidler, W. J. (1984) Creative Conflict Resolution. Scott, Foresman and Company.

Lawrence, D. (1973) Improved Reading Through Counselling. Ward Lock.

Maines, B. and Robinson, G. (1988) B/G-Steem. A Self-esteem Scale with Locus of Control items. Lucky Duck Publishing.

Maines, B. and Robinson, G. (1988) You can, You Know you can. Lucky Duck Publishing.

Maslow, A. (1968) Towards a Psychology of Being. Van Nostrand-Reinhold. New York.

Presland, J. (1996) Teaching pupils to negotiate. The Journal of the National Association for Pastoral Care and Personal and Social Education . Vol. 14 No.2.

Prutzman (1988) The Friendly Classroom for a Small Planet . Children's Creative Response to Conflict Program. New Society Publishers. New York.

Rogers, C.R. (1951) Client Centred Therapy - its current practices, implications and theory. Houghton Mifflin. Boston.
Scher, A. and Verrall, C. (1984) 100+ Ideas for Drama. Heinemann Educational Books. London.

Silcock, P., Stacey, H. and Wynas, M. (1997) Improving Social Competence: Peer Mediation in Birmingham Schools. Nene College, Park Campus, Northampton. NN2 7AL.

Stacey, H. (1996) Mediation into Schools Does Go : The Journal of Pastoral Care and Personal and Social Education. Vol.14. No. 2.

Stacey, H., Robinson, P. and Cremin, D. (1997) Using Conclict Resolution and Peer mediation to Tackle Bullying, in Tattum, D. and Herbert, H. (eds) Bullying in the Home, School and Community. David Fulton . London.

Thomas, K.W. and Kilmann,R. H. (1990) Thomas-Kilman Conflict Mode Instrument. Xicom Incorporated. Minnesota.

White, M. (1991) Self-esteem : Promoting Positive Practices for Responsible Behaviour, Circle Time strategies for Schools. Daniels Publishing.

Yeates, K.O. and Selman, R.L. (1989) Social Competence in Schools: Towards an Integrative Developmental Mode for Intervention. Developmental Review, Vol.9. No.1.

Yeates, K.O., Schulz, L.H. and Selman, R.L. (1991) The Development of Interpersonal Negotiation Strategies in Thought and Action : A Social-Cognitive Link to Behavioural Adjustment and Social Status. Merrill-Palmer Quarterly Vol. 37. No.3.

Addresses

The National Association for Pastoral Care in Education. c/o, Education Dept., University of Warwick, Coventry. CV4 7AL. Tel: 01202 523 810

The International Council for Self-esteem, 5, Ferry Path, Cambridge. CB4 1HB. Tel: 01223 - 65351

The Kingston Friends Workshop Group, Quaker Meeting House, 78, Eden Street, Kingston-upon-Thames, Surrey. KT1 1DJ. Tel: 0181 547 1197

Ulster Quaker Peace Education Project. c/o. The Centre for the Study of Conflict, University of Ulster, Coleraine, BT52 1SA.

LEAP Confronting Conflict Project, 8, Lennox Rd, Finsbury Park, London. N4 3NW. Tel: 0171 272 5630

Non-Violent Communication U.K. (The Language of Giraffe.) Forge House, Kemble, Gloucestershire. GL7 6AD

Mediation U.K. 82a Gloucester Road, Bishopston, Bristol. BS7 8BN Tel: 0117 924 1234

The Work of Catalyst Consultancy

The focus of Catalyst's work is promoting positive relationships and delivering consultancy and training in effective conflict resolution. Catalyst has worked in over 200 schools in the nursery, primary and secondary sector in different parts of the country. Hilary Stacey and Pat Robinson, Catalyst's business partners, work regularly in schools with both staff, parents and pupils in a variety of ways.

The careers that they had been following before establishing Catalyst in 1994 were, on the face of it, very different, but the values and visions held were very similar. Their interests spanned Theatre in Education, the World Studies movement, Development Education, Democratic Education, Equal Opportunities, Personal and Social Education, Community Education, Parent partnership and Anti-bullying work. What all of these have in common is the belief that all people, young and old, will flourish in an environment in which they feel valued and empowered, and a desire to create learning communities that facilitate this.

Hilary and Pat feel that the peer support and peer mediation work that they are currently developing offers a real, practical and structured way of reaching this goal. In this way they have been able to formalise something that they have been feeling their way towards for many years. We hope that other teachers reading this will feel the same way and that this book will go part of the way in helping others to reach their own goals.

Research and Publications

Catalyst has a strong research interest. Hilary Stacey is in the final stages of a Ph.D. which assesses the effectiveness of peer mediation, a developmental conflict resolution technique in which Hilary and Pat are national pioneers.

Informal research focuses on "emotional intelligence" (Goleman, 1996), effective behaviour management, and a social psychological approach to conflict resolution and pro-social skills training.

For more information about Catalyst Consultancy contact Pat Robinson & Hilary Stacey at 5, Cambridge Road, Kings Heath, Birmingham B13 9UE Tel: 0121 - 441 1222 Email : catalyst@stacerob.demon.co.uk

Circle Time

Circle Time, Developing Circle Time and the video, Coming Round to Circle Time are resources referenced in this publication. If you decide to buy the some or all of the materials they are available to you at a 10% discount.

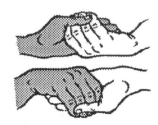

Please photocopy this page, completing the order form below, and send to

**Lucky Duck Publishing, 34, Wellington Park,
Clifton, Bristol BS8 2UW. Phone/Fax 0117 973 2881 or 01454 776620**

Name

Address

Postcode   **Date**   **Signed**

Order for:
___ **copy(ies) Circle Time @ £8**
___ **copy(ies) Developing Circle Time @ £9**
___ **copy(ies) Coming Round to Circle Time video @ £32 plus VAT £5.60**

Please add £1.00 towards postage

(10%) Discount for use in conjunction with Lets Mediate.